An Annotated
Critical Bibliography of
Augustan Poetry

Annotated Critical Bibliographies

This major new series provides extensive guides to literary movements and to major figures in English literature. Each volume is edited by a scholar of international repute, and writings by authors and the location of manuscript collections are presented in detail together with information on the secondary writings of each author.

Available

An Annotated Critical Bibliography of Modernism
Alistair Davies

An Annotated Critical Bibliography of Henry James
Nicola Bradbury

An Annotated Critical Bibliography of Milton
C. A. Patrides

An Annotated Critical Bibliography of Feminist Criticism
Maggie Humm

An Annotated Critical Bibliography of George Eliot
George Levine

An Annotated Critical Bibliography of James Joyce
Thomas Staley

An Annotated Critical Bibliography of Jacobean and Caroline Comedy
(excluding Shakespeare)
Peter Corbin and Douglas Sedge

An Annotated Critical Bibliography of Thomas Hardy
R. P. Draper and Martin Ray

An Annotated Critical Bibliography of Augustan Poetry
David Nokes and Janet Barron

An Annotated Critical Bibliography of Alfred Lord Tennyson
Marion Shaw

Forthcoming

An Annotated Critical Bibliography of Browning
Philip Drew

An Annotated Critical Bibliography of Langland
Derek Pearsall

An Annotated Critical Bibliography of William Morris
David and Sheila Latham

An Annotated Critical Bibliography of Virginia Woolf
Makiko Minow-Pinkney

An Annotated Critical Bibliography of Augustan Poetry

David Nokes

Reader in English Literature
King's College, London

Janet Barron

HARVESTER WHEATSHEAF

ST. MARTIN'S PRESS

First published 1989 by
Harvester Wheatsheaf,
66 Wood Lane End, Hemel Hempstead,
Hertfordshire, HP2 4RG
A division of
Simon & Schuster International Group

and in the USA by
St. Martin's Press Inc.
175 Fifth Avenue, New York, NY 10010

Printed and bound in Great Britain by
Billing and Sons Ltd, Worcester.

Library of Congress Cataloging-in-Publication Data

Nokes, David.
An annotated critical bibliography of Augustan poetry / David
Nokes. Janet Barron.
p. cm. — (annotated critical bibliographies)
Includes index.
ISBN 0–312–01961–0
1. English poetry—8th century—History and criticism—
Bibliography. 2. English poetry—Early modern. 1500–1700—History
and criticism—Bibliography. I. Barron, Janet. II. Title.
III. Series.
Z2014.P7N65 1989
[PR561]
016.821'509—dc20 89–10418
CIP

British Library Cataloguing in Publication Data

Nokes, David
An annotated critical bibliography of Augustan poetry –
(annotated critical bibliographies)
1. Poetry in English, 1625–1745. Bibliographies
I. Title II. Barron, Janet
016. 821'4

ISBN 0–7108–0972–7

---

1 2 3 4 5 93 92 91 90 89

Contents

Advice to the Reader

In parallel with other bibliographies in this series, the present volume has a twofold purpose. Part One provides an annotated bibliography of major books and articles dealing with the literary concept and context of Augustanism. And, since the term 'Augustanism' is itself a disputed one, this section expands to offer a full but selective bibliography of the most influential studies of English literature from Dryden to the pre-Romantic poets. In Part Two, the volume serves a second purpose by providing annotated bibliographies of all the leading eighteenth-century poets.

In selecting material for inclusion in this bibliography our principal aim has been to guide student readers through the accumulated mass of secondary studies that may confront them on the shelves of academic libraries or in the (unannotated) bibliographies of scholarly editions. Many of the works thus encountered will be once 'standard' studies that have subsequently been superseded, challenged or contradicted by later interpretations. We have attempted to alert our readers to such changes and developments in critical approaches. A large number of the works included fall within the broad category of 'liberal humanist' scholarship which has for several decades dominated the field of Augustan studies. But we also include representatives of many other critical approaches, ranging from the philological investigations of Susie Tucker (A27) to the feminism of Ellen Pollak (P59).

Part One, on the theme of Augustanism, is further divided into two subsections. The first of these deals with contextual and 'background' studies of the literature of the period. However, since the emphasis of this volume is on literature, only those works with a direct bearing on literary issues are included here. Thus a work of straightforward historical scholarship, such as J. H. Plumb's *Sir Robert Walpole* (London: 1956, 1960) is not included, but Bernard Goldgar's *Walpole and the Wits* (Lincoln, Nebraska: 1976; A47), which studies the relationship between politics and satire, is. Similarly, works dealing exclusively with eighteenth-century art and architecture are outside the scope of this volume, but those which discuss parallels between the literary and visual arts, such as Jean Hagstrum's *The Sister Arts* (Chicago and London: 1958; A10) are included.

The second section of Part One deals with general works on Augustan poetry, which should be consulted along with the author-specific studies noted in the individual entries in Part Two. As a further volume in the series will be devoted to Jonathan Swift, his poetry has been excluded from the present bibliography. It will be apparent that, in the authors we have selected, female names are underrepresented: this is not an attempt to perpetuate the marginalisation of women writers during this period, but reflects the fact that most female authors in the eighteenth century were novelists, and hence outside the range of this bibliography.

A principal difficulty arises with those authors for whom the writing of poetry represents only a minor element in their total *oeuvre*. Johnson is the most obvious example of this. A complete annotated bibliography of studies of Johnson would easily fill a book on its own. The *Philological Quarterly's Bibliography of Modern Studies of English Literature 1660–1800* lists 317 separate items on Johnson published during the decade 1961–70 alone. In the present bibliography therefore, in accordance with our overall purpose, we have limited ourselves to presenting only those studies which deal exclusively or mainly with Johnson's poetry. Works which are concerned with Johnson as a lexicographer, biographer or political writer, or with some specialist aspect of his prose writings, have not been included. Similar principles of selection have been applied to such authors as Addison and Burke. Burke's essay on *The Sublime and The Beautiful* (1757) had an important influence on literary and aesthetic theory and consequently studies of this aspect of his work are included. But his *Reflections on the Revolution in France* (1791), being a political work, falls outside the scope of this volume; and studies of it, and of his other political writings, are not included.

In general the works included in this bibliography have been chosen to reflect the development of critical debates, rather than as a comprehensive check-list of critical writings. Thus, for example, Arthur Friedman's edition of Goldsmith's *Works* (Oxford: 1966; GO1), with its critically conservative introduction, interprets Goldsmith as a sentimentalist, while Robert Hopkins's *The True Genius of Oliver Goldsmith* (Baltimore: 1969; GO11) offers a more radical reading of Goldsmith as a satirist. And, since commentators on Goldsmith's poetry often take their lead from critics of the novel, major studies of *The Vicar of Wakefield* are included to provide a context for understanding central critical issues.

Such distinctions are often difficult to make and may appear either arbitrary or ill-judged to some who consult this volume. However, apart from the simple constraints of space, we have always borne in mind that the principal users of this book are likely to be students of literature requiring a reliable guide to the most important studies of eighteenth-century poetry.

The number of entries for each author has also been a matter for careful selection. *Philological Quarterly's Bibliography of Modern Studies of English Literature 1660–1800* lists 276 separate items on Pope published during the 1960s, and it would clearly be possible to fill a whole book with an annotated bibliography of studies of his works alone. The present volume includes seventy entries on Pope which, we believe, offer a full and representative survey of all the most important and influential studies of his works from Joseph Warton's *Essay on the Genius and Writings of Pope* (London: 1756; P5) to the present day.

This bibliography is concerned with critical studies of Augustan literature, not with primary texts. Editions are included only when the editor's introduction to an author's works constitutes an important critical essay in its own right. In such cases our annotations refer only to the introductory essay and make no reference to the qualities – or otherwise – of the edition as a piece of textual scholarship.

David Nokes
Janet Barron
London 1989

Abbreviations

CAM Q	Cambridge Quarterly
ECS	Eighteenth-Century Studies
ELH	ELH, A Journal of Literary History
ELN	English Language Notes
HLQ	Huntington Library Quarterly
JEGP	Journal of English and Germanic Philology
MLR	Modern Language Review
MLQ	Modern Language Quarterly
MP	Modern Philology
PMLA	Publications of the Modern Language Association of America
PQ	Philological Quarterly
RES	Review of English Studies
SAQ	South Atlantic Quarterly
SEL	Studies in English Literature 1500–1900
SP	Studies in Philology
TSLL	Texas Studies in Language and Literature

Part One
Augustanism

The Augustan Context

Full-length studies of eighteenth-century literature and its cultural context. This section also includes collections of essays.

A1 Gosse, Edmund
A HISTORY OF EIGHTEENTH-CENTURY
LITERATURE 1660–1780 (London: 1889)

Along with Saintsbury's *The Peace of the Augustans* (A2), this is one of the classic studies of the literature of the period. Characteristically impressionistic and selective, it is better at highlighting some of the minor talents of the age such as Pomfret and Dyer, than at literary criticism. The language has a tone of pompous wit. Waller is described as 'the coryphaeus of this long procession of the commonplace'; *Windsor Forest* is described as 'a very promiscuous poem'. Interesting now only as an illustration of late-nineteenth-century attitudes to Augustan literature.

A2 Saintsbury, George
THE PEACE OF THE AUGUSTANS: A STUDY OF
EIGHTEENTH-CENTURY LITERATURE AS A PLACE
OF REST AND REFRESHMENT (London: 1916)

The subtitle says it all. Conversational and impressionistic, this stroll through Augustan literature enjoys such headings as 'Alexander Pope and his Kingdom'; 'The New Paradise of the Novel'; 'The Garden of Minor Verse'; and 'The Setting of the Augustan Sun'. Some shrewd observations among the chatter, but this is primarily a work of historical interest as representing a particular phase in literary criticism.

A3   Dyson, H. V. D. and John Butt
      AUGUSTANS AND ROMANTICS (London: 1940)

      A contextual study emphasising the links between 'literature'
      and 'life' and aiming 'to give the student some idea of the soil
      out of which the works of literature grew'. Worthy, but limited
      and subsequently superseded by several superior background
      and contextual studies.

A4   Willey, Basil
      THE EIGHTEENTH-CENTURY BACKGROUND
      (London: 1940; Penguin Books: 1962)

      For many years the standard 'background' study of the period
      used by generations of students. Offers succinct summaries of
      the works of philosophers from Thomas Burnet to Edmund
      Burke, with particularly useful sections on David Hume, Ber-
      nard Mandeville and Joseph Priestley. Throughout Willey uses
      changing concepts of Nature as his central theme, examining
      the idea of Nature in religion, ethics, philosophy and politics.
      This in itself is a strong indication of the kind of values and
      priorities that Willey cherishes in eighteenth-century literature.
      His study is less concerned with the Grub Street and coffee
      house milieu of eighteenth-century satire than with the process
      of the divinisation of Nature which culminated with
      Wordsworth.

A5   McKillop, Alan Dugald
      ENGLISH LITERATURE FROM DRYDEN TO BURNS
      (New York, London: 1948)

      Adopts a synoptic textbook approach with brief sketches of
      dozens of authors which are little more than biographical
      narratives. A few flashes of insight, but mainly rather dull and
      utilitarian.

A6   Butt, John
      THE AUGUSTAN AGE (London: 1950)

      Butt limits himself to presenting 'a few writers of paramount
      interest'. These are: Dryden, Addison, Swift, Pope, Thomson,

Collins, Shenstone, Gray and Johnson. The book is an interesting introduction with many sharp and perceptive points.

A7   Jack, Ian
     AUGUSTAN SATIRE: INTENTION AND IDIOM IN
     ENGLISH POETRY 1660–1750 (Oxford: 1952)

     A brief but perceptive and influential study of a select number
     of the better-known Augustan satires, from Butler's *Hudibras*
     to Johnson's *Vanity of Human Wishes*. Proceeding by a close
     analysis of the chosen texts, Jack offers a useful commentary on
     points of allusion, and on traditions of rhetoric and imitation.

A8   Humphreys, A. R.
     THE AUGUSTAN WORLD: LIFE AND LETTERS IN
     EIGHTEENTH-CENTURY ENGLAND (London: 1954)

     A sound and well-balanced 'background' book which continues
     to be of value despite the appearance of several rival works
     covering the same material in more recent years. Humphreys
     begins by declaring that 'the Augustan Age is noted for its sense
     of man as a social being'; thus his first chapter is devoted to
     'Social Life'. The other chapters deal with 'The World of
     Business', 'Public Affairs', 'Religious Life', 'Philosophy Moral
     and Natural' and 'The Visual Arts'. The book concludes with a
     series of reading lists still useful thirty-five years later.

A9   Ford, Boris (ed.)
     FROM DRYDEN TO JOHNSON, *The Pelican Guide to
     English Literature*, vol. IV (London: 1957; revised and
     expanded, 1982)

     This collection of essays presents an excellent study of eigh-
     teenth-century literature in its historical context.
     A. R. Humphreys provides useful introductory chapters on
     'The Social Setting' and 'The Literary Scene'. Thereafter a
     number of leading Augustan critics supply detailed studies of
     individual authors. Norman Callan has essays on Pope and on
     Augustan reflective poetry. Boris Ford writes on Goldsmith
     and D. J. Enright discusses Cowper. Other essays deal with
     literature and science (C. J. Horne), 'The Periodical Essayists'

(Jane H. Jack) and 'Books, Readers and Patrons' (Pat Rogers). A good introductory book for students.

A10   Hagstrum, Jean H.
THE SISTER ARTS (Chicago, London: 1958)

A detailed study of the pictorial element in poetry, and its expression in English verse from Dryden to Gray. Hagstrum is particularly interested in those images where a poet seems indebted to a particular painting or sculpture. Traces the classical tradition of *ut pictura poesis* from Plato to Lessing, but is mainly concerned with English neo-classicism. Judicious and learned.

A11   Røstvig, Maren-Sofie
THE HAPPY MAN, STUDIES IN THE METAMORPHOSES OF A CLASSICAL IDEAL, VOL. II, 1700–1760 (Oslo, Oxford: 1958)

This volume completes Røstvig's study of the classical motif of the *beatus vir* in English literature 1600–1760. She moves from Dryden's 'innocent epicureanism' to the more serious creed of bucolic bliss, celebrating the providential state of nature, in the 'happy gardener' poems of Pope, Shenstone and Lyttleton. Erudite and sharply focused. Røstvig's book is one of a number of studies emphasising the relationship between landscape gardening and literary theory in the Augustan period.

A12   Clifford, J. L. (ed.)
EIGHTEENTH-CENTURY ENGLISH LITERATURE: MODERN ESSAYS IN CRITICISM (New York: 1959)

An important collection of essays with some notable contributions by Maynard Mack and John Butt on Pope, C. S. Lewis on Addison and Bertrand Bronson on Johnson. Louis Bredvold's essay on 'The Gloom of the Tory Satirists' has acquired a classic status, as has Northrop Frye's essay on 'Defining An Age of Sensibility'. R. F. Jones, Marjorie Nicolson and Arthur Lovejoy contribute some interesting observations on the influence of science and philosophy on the literature of the period.

A13   Dobree, Bonamy
       ENGLISH LITERATURE IN THE EARLY
       EIGHTEENTH CENTURY, 1700–1740, *Oxford History of
       English Literature*, vol. vii (Oxford: 1959)

       A reference guide rather than a readable book, this useful
       volume provides an excellent context for understanding the
       background to the major writers. Among the central literary
       figures, Pope is given due prominence: Dobree looks at his
       'metaphysical' affinities, and offers a sympathetic reading of
       Windsor Forest, *Eloisa to Abelard* and the *Essay on Man*. There
       is also a wealth of material on the minor writers, and a non-
       specialist introduction to the moral philosophers including
       Berkeley and Shaftesbury.

A14   Lucas, Frank L.
       THE ART OF LIVING (London: 1959)

       Subtitled 'Four Eighteenth Century Minds', this is a study of
       Hume, Horace Walpole, Burke and Benjamin Franklin. 'The
       art of living' is Lucas' term for the 'balance' of 'civilized'
       qualities and 'good sense', in a period he defines as 'The Age of
       Reason'.

A15   Elliott, Robert C.
       THE POWER OF SATIRE: MAGIC, RITUAL, ART
       (Princeton: 1960)

       Examines the 'origins of satire in primitive magic and incanta-
       tion' as well as many of the major literary satires. Less con-
       cerned to offer literary interpretations of the works of such
       writers as Gay, Fielding or Congreve than to trace the surviving
       vestiges within their sophisticated satires of more ancient and
       atavistic energies. A useful discussion of Swift.

A16   Camden, Carroll (ed.)
       RESTORATION AND EIGHTEENTH-CENTURY
       LITERATURE: ESSAYS IN HONOUR OF ALAN
       DUGALD McKILLOP (Chicago, London: 1963)

       A fine and wide-ranging *Festschrift* whose twenty-nine essays
       include contributions by such leading Augustan scholars as
       Ehrenpreis, Sutherland and Tillotson.

A17   Price, Martin
TO THE PALACE OF WISDOM: STUDIES IN ORDER
AND ENERGY FROM DRYDEN TO BLAKE (New
York: 1964)

Another first-rate background book which stands alongside Pat
Roger's *Augustan Vision* (A44) as one of the most stimulating
contextual studies of the period for students of literature. The
pyrotechnic verbal style and Blakean title are typical of a
mid-1960s approach to the antithesis of order and energy.
Price's analysis of such individual authors as Dryden, Swift,
Pope, Gay, Fielding, Thomson and Blake are often brilliantly
original, though occasionally ostentatious.

A18   Foucault, Michel
MADNESS AND CIVILISATION: A HISTORY OF
INSANITY IN THE AGE OF REASON (1961) (trans.
Richard Howard) (New York: 1965)

Although most of Foucault's researches are based on French
sources, he also applies this study of madness and civilisation to
eighteenth-century English society. He concentrates on the
idea of the confinement of madmen as an Enlightenment
prejudice. His insights into the darker side of classical Augustan values have important implications for the study of many
literary works, including *The Dunciad* and *Gulliver's Travels*.

A19   Fussell, Paul
THE RHETORICAL WORLD OF AUGUSTAN
HUMANISM (Oxford: 1965)

Fussell's thesis is an interesting one: he attempts to describe
certain shared ethical convictions and related rhetorical techniques among six eighteenth-century writers – Swift, Pope,
Johnson, Reynolds, Gibbon and Burke. Without attempting to
force his chosen authors into a schematic model or theory, he
deduces underlying affinities from their shared fascination with
certain common pools of imagery. In chapters entitled 'Moral
Warfare: Strategy and Tactics'; 'The City of Life and the City of
Literature'; 'The Wardrobe of a Moral Imagination'; and 'The
Vermin of Nature', he examines the prevalence and significance of such images in their writings.

A20 Hilles, Frederick W. and Harold Bloom (eds.)
FROM SENSIBILITY TO ROMANTICISM: ESSAYS
PRESENTED TO FREDERICK A. POTTLE (New York:
1965)

This volume of essays contains interesting discussions of Pope,
Johnson, Collins and Gray. The general theme is the 'shift in
sensibility' during the second half of the eighteenth century
from 'Augustanism' to the Romantics. Some of the essays,
however, are of a more diverse nature: Maynard Mack contrib-
utes an essay on 'A Poet in his Landscape: Pope at
Twickenham', and W. K. Wimsatt discusses portraits of Pope.

A21 Kernan, Alvin B.
THE PLOT OF SATIRE (Yale: 1965)

Following his earlier study of satire in *The Cankered Muse*
(1959), Kernan sets out to discover a 'plot' or pattern in
Augustan satires which involves the ironic expansion and final
extinction of 'dullness'. Though the book ranges from Ben
Jonson to Evelyn Waugh, its central thesis treats *MacFlecknoe*,
The Rape of the Lock, *Trivia* and *The Dunciad*. Stimulating,
though with a tendency to become over-schematic.

A22 Wasserman, Earl (ed.)
ASPECTS OF THE EIGHTEENTH CENTURY
(Baltimore: 1965)

An interesting collection, containing useful essays by Maynard
Mack on Pope and the theme of retirement,
W. J. Bate on 'The English Poet and the Burden of the Past' and
Rene Wellek on 'The Term and Concept of Classicism'.

A23 Jones, William Powell
THE RHETORIC OF SCIENCE. A STUDY OF
SCIENTIFIC IDEAS AND IMAGERY IN
EIGHTEENTH-CENTURY ENGLISH POETRY (London:
1966)

Studies the influence of science on English poetry throughout
the eighteenth century, with particular attention to Pope,

Thomson, Akenside and Mallett. Also discusses a host of minor poets such as Henry Baker, Moses Browne, John Desaguliers, Bevill Higgon and Richard Jago, whose theological verses received fresh inspiration from the discoveries of the 'New Science'. Some overlap with Marjorie Nicolson's book *Newton Demands the Muse* (1946) (TH13).

A24   Malins, Edward
ENGLISH LANDSCAPING AND LITERATURE,
1660–1840 (London: 1966)

A synoptic study of the development of theories of landscape gardening, reflecting the aesthetic categories of the beautiful, the sublime and the picturesque. Fond of generalising theories, though some useful points on Pope and Shenstone.

A25   Johnson, James William
THE FORMATION OF NEO-CLASSICAL THOUGHT
(Princeton: 1967)

Begins by questioning the labels 'Augustan' and 'neo-classical' attached to the literature and criticism of the period. Studies in detail the influence of Hellenism on eighteenth-century scholarship and literature before examining the nature of the English admiration for the Augustan age of Rome. An interesting discussion of Byzantine influences precedes a chapter on Gibbon. Informative and scholarly, a useful source-book for students of literature and ideas.

A26   Paulson, Ronald
THE FICTIONS OF SATIRE (Baltimore: 1967)

Though more concerned with prose satires (especially with Swift) than with poetry, there is much stimulating material here for students of Dryden, Pope and Johnson. Paulson begins with the distinction between Horatian and Juvenalian satire, which he interprets as a difference between targeting the fool and the knave. A thoughtful and original work, though with a tendency to become over-schematic.

A27 Tucker, Susie I.
PROTEAN SHAPE: A STUDY IN EIGHTEENTH-
CENTURY VOCABULARY AND USAGES (London:
1967)

A detailed scholarly study of eighteenth-century vocabulary
written in a commendably unpedantic style. Tucker articulates
no new principles of linguistic change or development, but her
study is full of interesting and surprising details.

A28 Bronson, Bertrand H.
FACETS OF THE ENLIGHTENMENT: STUDIES IN
ENGLISH LITERATURE AND ITS CONTEXTS
(Berkeley, Los Angeles, London: 1968)

Bronson writes: 'The age was, as we now recognise, extraor-
dinarily complex'. In this series of essays he seeks to give some
sense of that complexity, visiting such little-frequented areas as
Prior's poetry, Gay's 'Acis and Galatea' and Percy's correspondence. He is equally interesting on more familiar territory, such
as the *Beggar's Opera*, Gray's *Elegy* and the Johnson/Boswell
relationship. Thoughtful and perceptive, these are the essays of
a man fascinated by the diversity and diversions of the eighteenth century.

A29 Clifford, James L.
MAN VERSUS SOCIETY IN EIGHTEENTH-CENTURY
BRITAIN: SIX POINTS OF VIEW (Cambridge: 1968)

A collection of symposium papers with a general bias towards
historical and political issues, though Bertrand Bronson's contribution on 'The Writer' is an interesting exploration of the
relationship between authors, patrons and readers.

A30 Harris, R. W.
REASON AND NATURE IN THE EIGHTEENTH
CENTURY (London: 1968)

A comprehensive if rather unimaginative background survey of
the period. Unlike Basil Willey (A4) or Pat Rogers (A44),
Harris offers no overall interpretation of eighteenth-century

ideas, but presents a series of self-contained chapters on various writers and philosophers. Useful in providing potted summaries of the works of such philosophers as Locke, Shaftesbury or Bishop Butler, though the summaries themselves are somewhat oversimplified.

A31   Marks, Emerson, R.
THE POETICS OF REASON: ENGLISH
NEOCLASSICAL CRITICISM (New York: 1968)

This study of English neo-classical criticism assumes two dimensions. The first is historical, setting critical concepts in their cultural contexts. The second is evaluative, assessing the strengths of neo-classical criticism in the light of subsequent literary values. After a brief but useful introductory section on the neo-classical 'rules', Marks concentrates on Dryden, Johnson, the concept of imitation, and neo-classical attitudes to Shakespeare.

A32   Donaldson, Ian
THE WORLD UPSIDE-DOWN: COMEDY FROM
JOHNSON TO FIELDING (Oxford: 1970)

Mainly concerned with dramatic comedy, but several points of interest for the student of poetry. An excellent combination of erudition, close analysis and thematic consistency takes Donaldson across the conventional boundaries of genre and period. Some sharp and witty criticism, as when *The Beggar's Opera* is described as 'a sentimental lollipop and a terse social fable'.

A33   Greene, Donald
THE AGE OF EXUBERANCE: BACKGROUNDS TO
EIGHTEENTH-CENTURY ENGLISH LITERATURE
(New York: 1970)

Argues that energy, rather than control, is the distinguishing feature of much eighteenth-century literature. Greene's own energetic style draws twentieth-century analogies to make eighteenth-century allusions and idioms more accessible. Echoing Johnson, Greene claims that 'though much is omitted, much has been performed'. A stimulating and often brilliant introduction to the period.

A34 Lipking, Lawrence
THE ORDERING OF THE ARTS IN EIGHTEENTH-
CENTURY ENGLAND (Princeton: 1970)

Traces the development of aesthetic theories during the century, relating to music, poetry and painting. Argues that no comprehensive theoretical history of these arts appeared until the writings of Reynolds (painting), Burney (music) and Johnson (poetry). Wide-ranging and detailed, though still selective in its exclusion of such popular forms as ballads, cartoons and burlesque comedy.

A35 Miller, Henry Knight, Eric Rothstein and G. S. Rousseau
(eds.)
THE AUGUSTAN MILIEU: ESSAYS PRESENTED TO
LOUIS A. LANDA (Oxford: 1970)

Largely concerned with history and politics, but Ehrenpreis has a lively and provocative essay on Pope, entitled 'The Style of Sound: The Literary Value of Pope's Versification'. In line with the argument of his book *Literary Meaning and Augustan Values* (A43), he suggests that the local effects of complex art may become 'ruinous to the rhetorical structure of the whole poem'. Arthur Friedman has an interesting essay on 'Aspects of Sentimentalism in Eighteenth Century Literature', and Charles Ryskamp discusses Smart's attempts to gain the patronage of the Earl of Northumberland.

A36 Foss, Michael
THE AGE OF PATRONAGE, THE ARTS IN ENGLAND
1660–1750 (Ithaca, New York: 1971)

A useful social history of the arts in England in the century following the Restoration. Foss describes the various dispensers of artistic patronage, firstly the Court, then the great lords of the revolutionary period, and finally the businessmen, lawyers and country gentry. He shows how the state of the arts fluctuated as it was affected by the waning influence of the King and Court, the rise of political parties and a new sense of middle-class decorum and responsibility.

A37   Hoyles, John
        THE EDGES OF AUGUSTANISM (The Hague: 1972)

As the subtitle explains, this is a study of 'the aesthetics of spirituality in Thomas Ken, John Byrom and William Law'. Essentially a thesis with a somewhat specialist appeal, it nevertheless casts some interesting light on relationships between religious faith and aesthetic principles in the eighteenth century.

A38   Rogers, Pat
        GRUB STREET, STUDIES IN A SUB-CULTURE
        (London: 1972)

A fascinating, informative and well-researched Baedeker to the world of Grub Street. Rogers documents the 'ecology of Dulness', examining the specific topos of Pope's dunces. He charts in detail the careers of such representative Grub Street figures as Oldmixon and Curll, rescuing them from the footnotes of literary history and placing them at the centre of his study. His aim throughout is to realise the metaphor of Grub Street, taking figures whose presentation in the *Dunciad* is often symbolic or representative, and analysing them as interesting literary subjects in their own right. Subsequently abridged as *Hacks and Dunces* (1980) (A52).

A39   Elkin, P. K.
        THE AUGUSTAN DEFENCE OF SATIRE (Oxford: 1973)

Elkin examines a range of Augustan attitudes to satire, ranging from Pope, who saw it as a 'sacred weapon', to Addison, who regarded it as a cowardly 'secret stab'. He discriminates between Horatian and Juvenalian satire, smiling and snarling satire, raillery and railing. He concludes that satire was 'killed by kindness', in other words by the sentimental novel.

A40   Byrd, Max
        VISITS TO BEDLAM: MADNESS AND LITERATURE
        IN THE EIGHTEENTH CENTURY (Columbia,
        S. Carolina: 1974)

Unlike the ancient Greeks, for whom madness could be a divine symbol, Byrd argues that Pope, Swift and Johnson treat insanity with satiric contempt. By the century's end, however, madness takes on once again an inspired attraction (as in Blake's work). A lively but partial account, heavily influenced by Foucault (A18).

A41   Battestin, Martin C.
THE PROVIDENCE OF WIT: ASPECTS OF FORM IN AUGUSTAN LITERATURE AND THE ARTS (Oxford: 1974)

Battestin insists on the continuity of Augustan ideals with the Christian humanism of the Renaissance. He argues that firm intellectual and moral assumptions determine the forms and images of literature and art. Sometimes his insistence on such absolute moral abstractions as order or providence underlying the playful satire seems unnecessarily didactic, introducing certain thematic and schematic simplifications. But this is an important ideological reinterpretation of the age, bearing a comparison with Fussell's *The Rhetorical World of Augustan Humanism* (A19).

A42   De Porte, Michael V.
NIGHTMARES AND HOBBYHORSES: SWIFT, STERNE AND AUGUSTAN IDEAS OF MADNESS (San Marino, California: 1974)

Although mainly devoted to Swift and Sterne, this intriguing analysis of theories of insanity in the 'Age of Reason' will be of interest to all students of the literature of the period. Discussion of eighteenth-century medical and psychological theories of madness is used to explain attitudes to the imagination.

A43   Ehrenpreis, Irvin
LITERARY MEANING AND AUGUSTAN VALUES (Charlottesville, Virginia: 1974)

An important if brief volume which questions some critical assumptions about the role and significance of imitation and allusion in Augustan literature. Emphasising the importance of explicitness in Augustan literature, Ehrenpreis argues that 'Allusion as such can decorate handsomely: it cannot deepen'.

A44   Rogers, Pat
       THE AUGUSTAN VISION (London: 1974)

One of the best background studies of the period. Rogers
begins with a hundred-page discussion of 'The Landscape of the
Age'. Rejecting Saintsbury's description of the age in *The
Peace of the Augustans* (1916) (A2) as an elegant era of rest,
refinement and refreshment, Rogers concentrates on the Janus-
faced contradictions of eighteenth-century society. 'It was a
period when humanitarian zeal was abundant, as instanced by
the foundation of five major hospitals . . . but this was also a
period when capital offences mounted towards the two hundred
mark'. His short critical sections on each of the major authors
are sharp, lively and perceptive. He conveys a wealth of
information and a subtlety of insight in a style which is witty,
terse and full of vigour.

A45   Hunt, John Dixon and Peter Willis
       THE GENIUS OF THE PLACE: THE ENGLISH
       LANDSCAPE GARDEN 1620–1820 (London: 1975)

Lavishly illustrated, this anthology of over fifty authors from
Henry Wotten to Peacock is a survey of tastes and theories
concerning 'hortulan pleasures'.

A46   Maresca, Thomas E.
       EPIC TO NOVEL (Columbus, Ohio: 1975)

An interesting if somewhat provocative and schematic attempt
to trace the transformation of the 'true' epic into the 'comic epic
in prose'. The chosen authors for special study are Dryden,
Pope, Swift and Fielding.

A47   Goldgar, Bernard A.
       WALPOLE AND THE WITS: THE RELATION OF
       POLITICS TO LITERATURE, 1722–42 (Lincoln,
       Nebraska: 1976)

Examining both the well-known and the unfamiliar political
satires of the period, Goldgar gives a picture of the relationship
between literature and politics of interest to both the scholar
and the general reader. Particularly useful is its presentation of

material from such neglected journals as *Fog's Journal*, *The Craftsman* and *The Jacobites Journal*. Concerned with 'individual careers and concrete events rather than with political ideology'.

A48   Hilson, J. C., M. M. B. Jones and J. R. Watson (eds.)
AUGUSTAN WORLDS (New York: 1978)

An interesting collection of essays in honour of A. R. Humphreys. There are four essays, by Ian Jack, Maynard Mack, Pat Rogers and George Fraser on aspects of Pope's life and works. Lois Potter has a lively piece on Cibber (CI7). Most of the other essays are on Swift or the novelists.

A49   Rogers, Pat (ed.)
THE EIGHTEENTH CENTURY, Methuen *Contexts of English Literature* series (London: 1978)

An imaginative and enterprising background book which offers five wide-ranging, lengthy and distinctive essays, each by a specialist contributor, on different aspects of eighteenth-century culture. Rogers himself writes on 'The Writer and Society', traversing some of the same territory covered in *Grub Street* (1972) (A38) and *The Augustan Vision* (1974) (A44). W. A. Speck offers a brisk and balanced account of eighteenth-century politics from the reign of Queen Anne to the rise of the Younger Pitt. J. V. Price examines religion and philosophy, G. S. Rousseau analyses the role and influence of science, and Peter Willis discusses the visual arts. All of the essays are well written, achieving a sound balance of comprehensive outline and illuminating detail. An excellent contextual study.

A50   Ehrenpreis, Irvin
ACTS OF IMPLICATION (Berkeley, Los Angeles, London: 1980)

Subtitled 'Suggestion and Covert Meaning in the Works of Dryden, Swift, Pope and Austen'. Ehrenpreis sets out to show 'that subtlety and indirection do not by their nature work against didacticism or an apparently lucid style'. He demonstrates a rich, ironic blend of explicit and implicit meanings in his chosen authors.

A51   Landa, Louis A.
ESSAYS IN EIGHTEENTH-CENTURY LITERATURE
(Princeton: 1980)

A collection of reprinted articles by Landa, from 1942 to 1975,
together with a brief introduction. The first seven essays are
concerned with Swift; among the remaining six, essays on
Rasselas and *The Rape of the Lock* will be of interest to students
of Augustanism. In the latter essay, Landa puts Belinda's
materialist values in the context of economic and social theory.

A52   Rogers, Pat
HACKS AND DUNCES: POPE, SWIFT AND GRUB
STREET (London, New York: 1980)

In this abbreviated paperback revision of his earlier *Grub Street*
(1972) (A38), Rogers sharpens the focus and heightens the
concentration of his argument. Less meandering down Grubian
alley-ways; more emphasis on the metaphorical centres of
Bedlam, Smithfield and Newgate.

A53   Porter, Roy
ENGLISH SOCIETY IN THE EIGHTEENTH CENTURY,
The Pelican Social History of Britain (London: 1982)

An immensely readable and well-informed book. Porter writes
in a vivid, colourful yet relaxed style, with a flair for highlighting
the contrasts and ironies of the period. A historian not afraid to
use literature and art, as well as economics and demography, to
complete his social analysis. Sometimes breathless, crammed
with detail, it is an excellent introduction to the period.

A54   Rogers, Katherine M.
FEMINISM IN EIGHTEENTH-CENTURY ENGLAND
(Brighton: 1982)

Though less comprehensive than the title suggests, this is a
useful analysis of the presentation of female experience in the
works of both male and female authors. Rogers often jux-
taposes scenes from texts by male and female authors to
illustrate their sex-based assumptions.

A55 Sheriff, John K.
THE GOOD-NATURED MAN: THE EVOLUTION OF A
MORAL IDEAL, 1600–1800 (Alabama: 1982)

Very much a thesis. Sheriff believes that 'for every student of
literature a knowledge of the good-natured Man type will
provide insights into the art and ethics of eighteenth century
English literature'. This book, however, is too narrowly
focused to provide many such insights.

A56 Carretta, Vincent
THE SNARLING MUSE, VERBAL AND VISUAL
SATIRE FROM POPE TO CHURCHILL (Philadelphia:
1983)

This is mainly a study of Pope's satires, with copious analogies
and cross-references to the visual lampoons of the period. Well-
informed, intelligent and perceptive. The attempt to say something about the decline of satire in the later eighteenth century
is to be welcomed, though here Carretta promises more than he
delivers.

A57 Barrell, John
ENGLISH LITERATURE IN HISTORY 1730–1780, AN
EQUAL, WIDE SURVEY (London: 1983)

Aims to describe how writers of the period 'attempted to
construct an understanding of contemporary social changes'.
His 'equal, wide survey' takes in the social views of Pope,
Mandeville, Steele, Thomson, Defoe, Dyer, Johnson and
Smollett, among others.

A58 Novak, Maximillian E.
EIGHTEENTH-CENTURY ENGLISH LITERATURE
(London: 1983)

Examines the familiar antitheses of eighteenth-century literature through his own form of dialectical analysis, contrasting
fancy's maze with social realism, and sentiment with moral
earnestness. Useful to students in its contextual discussion of
such subjects as Locke's philosophy and neo-classical art.

A59   Speck, W. A.
SOCIETY AND LITERATURE IN ENGLAND 1700–60
(London: 1983)

An interesting and enterprising book offering a new perspective on the interrelationships between literature and society. This is a work not of sociology but of iconography, since Speck does not examine eighteenth-century society itself, but rather the contrasting images of that society presented in its literature. There are particularly interesting discussions of the image of the Tory squire, the Wheel of Fortune and of the contrast between town and country values.

A60   Bogel, Fredric V.
LITERATURE AND INSUBSTANTIALITY IN LATER
EIGHTEENTH-CENTURY ENGLAND (Princeton: 1984)

Bogel argues that 'English writers in the Age of Sensibility were, to a surprising degree, united by a perception of the impoverishment or insubstantiality of their experience'. A chapter on Johnson describes the attempt to find meaning in the defence of common experience. Other chapters deal with rhetorical appeals to the past and present.

A61   Kenny, Virginia C.
THE COUNTRY HOUSE ETHOS IN ENGLISH
LITERATURE, 1688–1750 (Brighton, New York: 1984)

Kenny's book studies the interrelated themes of individual retreat and national expansion in such poems as *Windsor Forest* and *The Seasons*. In this way she puts the literary theme of Horatian retirement into a broader context as a response to social and political changes. An interesting book, which uses its specific theme to open out intriguing perspectives on a range of eighteenth-century texts, from *Robinson Crusoe* to *The Castle of Indolence*.

A62   Nussbaum, Felicity A.
THE BRINK OF ALL WE HATE, ENGLISH SATIRES
ON WOMEN, 1660–1750 (Lexington, Kentucky: 1984)

A witty feminist study of anti-feminist wit. Nussbaum's book documents and categorises Restoration and Augustan satires on women in order to isolate the literary conventions which contribute to the creation of recognisable satiric 'myths'. She also provides critical readings of selected poetic texts and offers some general thoughts on the nature of satire.

A63   Rawson, Claude (ed.)
ENGLISH SATIRE AND THE SATIRIC TRADITION
(Oxford: 1984)

Although the essays in this volume range from Aristophanes to Borges, there is a concentration on the Augustan satirists. Raman Selden documents Pope's borrowings from Oldham; Howard Erskine-Hill examines the political significance of the card games in *The Rape of the Lock*; Niall Rudd offers a series of notes on Pope's *Imitations of Horace*.

A64   Patey, Douglas Lane and Timothy Keegan (eds.)
AUGUSTAN STUDIES: ESSAYS IN HONOUR OF
IRVIN EHRENPREIS (Toronto: 1985)

Includes an interesting essay by Emrys Jones on Dryden's translations of Lucretius.

A65   Rawson, Claude
ORDER FROM CONFUSION SPRUNG: STUDIES IN
EIGHTEENTH-CENTURY LITERATURE FROM
SWIFT TO COWPER (London: 1985)

An excellent, lively series of essays by this outstanding Augustan scholar. Instead of the conventional reference back to Homer, Virgil, Horace and Juvenal, Rawson's favourite movement is forward, uncovering parallels with Conrad and Yeats, Malamud and Mailer. Attacking the 'vulgar philistinism' which treats Augustan literature as a 'sealed unit', he offers a view of eighteenth-century literature which emphasises its modernity, its disturbing force and its moral relevance.

A66   Rogers, Pat
EIGHTEENTH CENTURY ENCOUNTERS: STUDIES IN
LITERATURE AND SOCIETY IN THE AGE OF
WALPOLE (Brighton: 1985)

A fascinating volume of essays by this leading Augustan scholar, examining some of the less-frequented byways of cultural study. Rogers declares that 'events fascinate me more than ideology', and his book is full of factual details reflecting the great variety of eighteenth-century literature and society. Interesting essays on Pope's *Rambles* and on Pope's attitude to the Waltham Black Act of 1723.

A67   Rogers, Pat
LITERATURE AND POPULAR CULTURE IN
EIGHTEENTH-CENTURY ENGLAND (Brighton: 1985)

Like the preceding volume, this is a collection of lively, quirky essays, concentrating on the ways in which popular culture permeates the mock-heroic literature of the age. Three essays on *The Dunciad* illustrate the role and significance of the City poet Elkanah Settle, the satire on Italian opera and the parody of the coronation of George II.

A68   Lonsdale, Roger (ed.)
DRYDEN TO JOHNSON, *The Sphere History of Literature*,
vol. 4 (London: 1971; revised 1986)

An excellent introduction to the literature of the period, with essays by leading eighteenth-century scholars. Includes Erskine-Hill on Dryden, F. W. Bateson on Addison and Steele, Lonsdale on Pope, and David Nokes on Sterne.

A69   Nokes, David
RAILLERY AND RAGE, A STUDY OF EIGHTEENTH-
CENTURY SATIRE (Brighton: 1987)

A guide, for modern readers, to the teasing paradoxes and allusive parodies of eighteenth-century satire. Nokes suggests a number of general strategies for evaluating the significance of literary allusions and for understanding the effects of such literary techniques as irony, parody, mock-heroism and burlesque. The book begins with some general observations on the ideological assumptions, themes and forms of Augustan satire. This is followed by four chapters analysing representative satires by Pope, Gay, Fielding and Swift.

A70 Nussbaum, Felicity and Laura Brown (eds.)
THE NEW EIGHTEENTH CENTURY: THEORY,
POLITICS, ENGLISH LITERATURE (New York,
London: 1987)

The editors of this volume of essays offer a direct challenge to
the liberal–humanist consensus which, in their view, has both
dominated and narrowed the study of eighteenth-century literature and society. They argue that the writings of such influential critics as Reuben Brower (P17) and Earl Wasserman (P18,
A22) have perpetuated the notion of the eighteenth century as a
'tranquil haven of political stability' while marginalising or
ignoring the voices of dissent in the period. Such liberal–
humanist critics, they claim, have been mainly concerned with
'the preservation and elucidation of canonical masterpieces of
cultural stability'. By contrast, the contributors to this volume
share a belief that 'the most important work always insists on
the relations between ideology, gender, race and class, and on
the functions of the oppressed and excluded in texts and
cultural formations'. Essays in the volume focus on the roles
and literary representation of women, servants and slaves.
Laura Brown offers an essay on '*Oroonoko* and the Trade in
Slaves'; John Richetti examines 'Servants and Proletarians in
Fielding and Smollett'; Terry Castle investigates 'The Spectral-
ization of the Other in *The Mysteries of Udolpho*'; and Carole
Fabricant discusses 'The Literature of Domestic Tourism'. Jill
Campbell, Donna Landry and Felicity Nussbaum offer essays
on various aspects of the politics of gender. This is a stimulating
and controversial book, which invites a complete reassessment
of many traditional assumptions about eighteenth-century
culture.

Eighteenth-century Poetry

This section includes full-length general studies of eighteenth-century poetry, as well as discussions of changes and developments in poetic theory and practice during the period.

A71   Johnson, Samuel
THE LIVES OF THE ENGLISH POETS (London: 1779, 1781)

A classic work of literary criticism, still offering some of the sharpest and most sensitive insights into the works of a wide range of seventeenth- and eighteenth-century poets. Commissioned as a set of introductions to a collection of the English poets, the lives range from such major poets as Milton, Dryden and Pope to such forgotten figures as Pomfret, Stepney and Yalden. Although the main emphasis of the *Lives* is biographical, each essay includes a useful and often magisterial section of critical evaluation. Johnson's dislike of novelty, demonstrated in his life of Cowley, and of pastoral, as seen in his lives of Gay and Lyttleton, are well known. His emphasis throughout is on truth to nature. Many of his judgements have become the essential starting-points for subsequent critical debates. His remark on Gray: 'He has a kind of strutting dignity, and is tall by walking on tip-toe'; or on Thomson: 'The great defect of *The Seasons* is want of method', would be good examples. Intelligent, judicious, forthright and readable, it remains one of the few indispensable critical studies of the poetry of the period. See separate entries for Pope (P67) and Gay (G12).

A72   Deane, C. V.
ASPECTS OF EIGHTEENTH-CENTURY NATURE POETRY (Oxford: 1935)

Deane aims to provide 'a fresh estimate of the positive values of neo-classic and pre-romantic nature poetry'. He differentiates between nature poetry which is merely a 'lifeless' use of convention, and poetry which has been 'inspired' by a personal response to the subject. The authors he covers include William Shenstone, Ambrose Philips and Alexander Pope.

A73 Peltz, Catharine Walsh
THE NEO-CLASSIC LYRIC 1660–1725 (Baltimore: 1944)

A very brief dissertation attempting to describe a tradition.

A74 Brown, Wallace Cable
THE TRIUMPH OF FORM: A STUDY OF THE LATER MASTERS OF THE HEROIC COUPLET (Chapel Hill, N. Carolina: 1948)

An interesting study in both form and content, tracing the development and variation in uses of the couplet. There are separate chapters on Gay, Johnson, Churchill, Young, Cowper, Goldsmith and Crabbe. Intelligent and subtle.

A75 Sutherland, James
A PREFACE TO EIGHTEENTH-CENTURY POETRY (Oxford: 1948)

A self-consciously pioneering work to 'remove some of the obstacles which impede the modern reader's enjoyment of eighteenth century poetry'. Elegantly written, combining a wealth of knowledge with judicious and perceptive literary insights. More emphasis on refinement and restraint than would be fashionable now, but still a useful, readable conspectus.

A76 Arthos, John
THE LANGUAGE OF NATURAL DESCRIPTION IN EIGHTEENTH-CENTURY POETRY (Ann Arbor, Michigan: 1949)

A study of the 'stock diction' of eighteenth-century English poetry, and in particular of 'the diction commonly used in the description of nature'. Explores the relationship between the language of nature poetry and the vocabulary of the natural philosophers.

A77   Congleton, J. E.
THEORIES OF PASTORAL POETRY IN ENGLAND,
1684–1798 (Gainesville, Florida: 1952)

The classic study of the development and tradition of pastoral
poetry as transmitted from Renaissance times to the Augustan
period. Congleton discriminates with skill between the various
forms and tones of pastoral: idyll, eclogue, bucolic, georgic, as
well as mock-eclogues, town-eclogues and the many satiric
variations on pastoral themes. He offers a narrative and formal-
ist account of changing attitudes towards pastoral, from con-
sciously literary neo-classical artifice to the Romantic
rediscovery of the simplicities of the shepherd's life.

A78   Chapin, C. F.
PERSONIFICATION IN EIGHTEENTH-CENTURY
ENGLISH POETRY (New York: 1955)

Chapin approaches the use of personifications as an aspect of
the wider patterns of contemporary literary theories. He distinguishes between two kinds of personified abstraction: the
figure visualised in the imagination as an allegorical embodiment, and the more 'metaphoric' personification which gives
poetic value to statements of general truth. The second type of
personification is, Chapin argues, closely related to the poetic
theories of Pope and Johnson.

A79   Davie, Donald (ed.)
THE LATE AUGUSTANS, *Poetry Bookshelf* series
(London: 1958)

An important anthology, demonstrating the vitality and continuity of English lyrical poetry throughout the eighteenth
century. A persuasive and interesting introduction presents
Wordsworth as a 'late Augustan' and offers an alternative
poetic tradition, including such writers as Gray, Smart and
Shenstone, to the satiric style of Dryden, Pope and Johnson.

A80   Williamson, George
THE PROPER WIT OF POETRY (London, Chicago: 1961)

Essentially a study of the development of 'wit' in poetry, and of
the concept of wit itself, during the seventeenth century. Begin-

ning with some remarks on Elizabethan rhetoric and Jacobean paradoxes, Williamson proceeds chronologically via metaphysical conceits to the antithetical wit of Dryden and the Augustan satirists. Examining the Augustans, Williamson notes how the wit of contradiction is contained within the wit of resemblance.

A81   Spacks, Patricia Meyer
THE INSISTENCE OF HORROR: ASPECTS OF THE
SUPERNATURAL IN EIGHTEENTH-CENTURY
POETRY (Harvard: 1962)

While acknowledging that much of the crepuscular and charnel-house verse that she has examined for this study is 'poor stuff', Spacks cheerfully analyses themes and theories, diction and devices. She also discusses a range of eighteenth-century attitudes to the supernatural, from rational condescension to sensationalism and sentimentality. Offers an interesting though glimmering sidelight on the poetry of the period.

A82   Lord, George De F.
POEMS ON AFFAIRS OF STATE: AUGUSTAN
SATIRICAL VERSE 1660–1714 (Yale: 1963)

A fascinating compilation of political satires, mainly remarkable for the inclusion of a teeming variety of anonymous and pseudonymous broadsheets, ballads and scurrilous lampoons. Provides an excellent context for the better-known verse satires of Dryden, Rochester and Pope.

A83   Buxton, John
A TRADITION OF POETRY (London: 1967)

Covers eight poets from Wyatt to the later eighteenth century. Of interest to students of Augustanism are the essays on the following:

1. Lady Winchilsea ('Women are education's and not Nature's fools' – Buxton claims Winchilsea's poetry as the first that only a woman could have written).
2. Waller, whose characteristics of elegance and gaiety are 'not so common with us that we can afford their neglect'.

A84   Peake, Charles (ed.)
POETRY OF THE LANDSCAPE AND THE NIGHT
(London: 1967)

In this brief but illuminating anthology, Peake presents two
eighteenth-century verse traditions. In the landscape tradition
he notes the mingled effects of Virgilian imagery and topographical references. In the nocturnal tradition, echoes of
Milton's *Il Penseroso* merge into melancholy meditations. Offers examples from twenty-four poets, from Denham and Dyer
to Akenside and Burns.

A85   Spacks, Patricia Meyer
THE POETRY OF VISION: FIVE EIGHTEENTH-
CENTURY POETS (Cambridge, Mass.: 1967)

A detailed examination and aesthetic comparison of the image
patterns of Thomson, Collins, Gray, Smart and Cowper.

A86   Trickett, Rachel
THE HONEST MUSE: A STUDY IN AUGUSTAN
VERSE (Oxford: 1967)

Trickett claims that her book 'is not in any sense an exhaustive
study of Augustan poetry' and her central emphasis is on the
poetry of Dryden, Pope and Johnson, which she examines 'in
relation to the political and intellectual circumstances in which
they worked'. While her study of retirement, benevolence and
the joys of a simple life invoke all the attitudes usually labelled
'Horatian', she herself prefers the designation of the 'Honest
Muse' to indicate a specifically English strain of panegyric,
satire and elegy. In her study of the poetic presentation of town
versus country attitudes, she illustrates Pope's debt, both in
imagery and ethics, to the Restoration poets Cowley, Oldham,
Rochester and Dryden. An excellent, lucid and persuasive
book.

A87   Chalker, John
THE ENGLISH GEORGIC: A STUDY IN THE
DEVELOPMENT OF A FORM (Baltimore: 1969)

Argues that the georgic was eminently suited to presenting
multiple viewpoints, particularly those implicit in mock-heroic.

Contrasts Addison, who regarded the form as part of the science of husbandry, with Gay, who developed it for a range of comic and satiric purposes. Makes sensible and interesting distinctions between a georgic tradition and the more general influence of pastoral.

A88 Heath-Stubbs, John
THE VERSE SATIRE, THE ODE, THE PASTORAL
(Oxford: 1969), 3 vols.

Using a historical approach, each of these brief introductions traces the origins of these poetic forms back to Greek literature and discusses their subsequent evolution. Descriptive and formal rather than critical in method.

A89 Piper, William Bowman
THE HEROIC COUPLET (Case Western Reserve
University Press: 1969)

A study of the development of the couplet from Chaucer to Keats, though the most important chapters deal with Denham, Dryden and Pope. Some questionable quasi-historical assertions about the pressures of 'societal unrest' in the seventeenth century inducing a need for a 'stricter adherence to unquestioned principles' in the form of closed couplets. Sounder in his close textual readings of selected couplets than in his larger historical generalisations.

A90 Weinbrot, Howard D.
THE FORMAL STRAIN: STUDIES IN AUGUSTAN
IMITATION AND SATIRE (Chicago: 1969)

A scholarly study of the traditions of the genre of verse satire imitation from Denham to Johnson. Weinbrot's attention is fairly narrowly focused on imitations of Juvenal and Horace, without deviating into some of the less conventional mock-heroic forms of parodic imitation. A learned and informative work, though occasionally over-schematic.

A91 Bate, Walter Jackson
THE BURDEN OF THE PAST AND THE ENGLISH
POET (Cambridge, Mass.: 1970)

Argues that a sense of the past became more of a burden than a boon for late-eighteenth-century poets as imitation gave way to originality as a dominant ideal. Examines the ambivalent influence of the past on a range of authors who are both nurtured and inhibited by the literary models of their predecessors.

A92   Korshin, Paul J.
FROM CONCORD TO DISSENT, MAJOR THEMES IN ENGLISH POETIC THEORY 1640–1700 (London: 1973)

The principal concern of this book is the examination of theories of English poetry from 1640 to 1700. Includes two chapters on Dryden. The first provides an excellent reading of *Absalom and Achitophel*, uncovering a triple-layered structure of biblical narrative, political allusions, and an allegory of 'a crisis of unreason' in the intellectual sphere which mirrors a constitutional crisis. In the second chapter Korshin suggests that Dryden became increasingly defensive in later life, turning away from the public statements of his earlier works.

A93   Davie, Donald (ed.)
AUGUSTAN LYRIC, *Poetry Bookshelf* series (London: 1974)

Following on from his volume *The Late Augustans* (1958) (A79), Davie continues to point out the varieties and idiosyncrasies of poetic expression available within the 'Augustan' idiom. In *Augustan Lyric* he celebrates Isaac Watts but not, interestingly, as a way of disparaging better-known Augustan values. 'Isaac Watts', he writes, 'is a great poet by precisely those standards that make Pope a great poet'. Davie devotes more space to four poets (Watts, Smart, Cowper, John Newton) 'whose genius was indeed lyrical, to a degree that . . . is still unacknowledged'. At times the label 'Augustan' seems rather awkward and empty in this context, but the volume is a fine introduction to the diversity of poetic voices and styles in the period.

A94   Rothstein, Eric
RESTORATION AND EIGHTEENTH-CENTURY POETRY 1660–1780, *The Routledge History of English Poetry* (London: 1981)

An intelligent historical guide, neither modish nor pedantic, offering sensible judgements and sound descriptions. Includes a useful chronological analysis as an appendix.

A95   Doody, Margaret Anne
       THE DARING MUSE, AUGUSTAN POETRY
       RECONSIDERED (Cambridge: 1985)

'Too much talk about "decorum" and "correctness" can only depress the uninitiated', writes Doody, who in this reconsideration of eighteenth-century poetry wishes to emphasise instead 'the excitement of the works, and their strangeness'. Broadening the range of 'Augustan' writers, she includes more Dissenters, women, provincial and 'minor' poets than is usual in such studies. Her book is also richly illustrated. An important work in opening out the study of Augustan poetry. Diversity, curiosity and energy are the qualities that fascinate her, though she does not lose sight of the more familiar neo-classical preoccupations with order, virtue and the good life.

Periodicals and shorter articles

A96   Dobree, Bonamy
       'The Theme of Patriotism in the Poetry of the Early
       Eighteenth Century', Warton Lecture on English Poetry
       (London: 1949)

Thomson is the main poet discussed, along with Prior, Glover, Philips, Dyer and Tickell.

A97   Frye, Northrop
       'Towards Defining an Age of Sensibility', *ELH* xxiii (1956)
       144–52 (reprinted in *Eighteenth-Century English Literature*,
       ed. J. L. Clifford (A12) 311–18)

Suggests that the work of such 'post-Augustan' poets as Chatterton and Smart is characterised by 'an interest in the poetic process as distinct from the product'. Theirs is an oracular poetry of dreamlike free-association in which 'rhyme is as important as reason'.

A98   Greene, Donald
       'Augustinianism and Empiricism: A Note on Eighteenth-
       Century Intellectual History', *Eighteenth-Century Studies* 1
       (1967) 33–68

       A provocative assault on the time-worn phrases 'Augustan',
       'Age of Reason' and 'Neo-classical' used to designate eigh-
       teenth-century literature. The period, Greene argues, might as
       usefully be termed 'Augustinian' as 'Augustan'. He provides
       some corroborative evidence, but this is mainly a skilful ex-
       ercise in scholarly debating, intended to question lazy
       assumptions.

A99   Miner, Earl
       'From Narrative to "Description" and "Sense" in
       Eighteenth-Century Poetry', *SEL* ix (1969) 471–87

       Sees a gradual move away from the centrality of narrative or
       plot towards sentiment and description in the poetry of the
       period. Pope, Thomson, Akenside, Gray, Blair, Goldsmith,
       Johnson and Cowper are all discussed.

A100   Sitter, John E.
       'Theodicy at Mid-century: Pope, Akenside and Hume', *ECS*
       12 (1978) 90–106

       Argues that Young's *Night Thoughts* and Akenside's *The Plea-
       sures of Imagination* have more in common with each other
       than with Pope's *Essay on Man*.

Part Two
Studies of Individual Poets

Addison and Steele

Addison, Joseph (1672–1719)

Full-length Studies

AS1   Macaulay, Lord T. B.
THE LIFE AND WRITINGS OF ADDISON, *Critical and Historical Essays, English Library* Series (London: 1907)

For long the standard biography, Macaulay's work should now be consulted with more recent criticism, as modern scholarship has shown many of his conclusions to be inaccurate.

AS2   Smithers, Peter
THE LIFE OF JOSEPH ADDISON (Oxford: 1954)

A well-researched narrative of Addison's life, though the emphasis is less on the man than on the politician. Smithers sets Addison's political career and journalism in the context of the early-eighteenth-century history of the Whigs and Tories, demonstrating the fluid beginnings of party allegiance in a prevailing spirit of liberal humanism.

AS3   Elioseff, L. A.
THE CULTURAL MILIEU OF ADDISON'S LITERARY CRITICISM (Austin: 1963)

Elioseff examines the historical setting of Addison's criticism, and concentrates on Addison's theories in relation to ballad, epic and tragedy. A useful approach to Addison's poetic theories.

AS4   Bloom, Edward and Lillian
JOSEPH ADDISON'S SOCIABLE ANIMAL (Providence,
Rhode Island: 1971)

An account of Addison's work which attempts to establish a
coherent philosophy in his twenty-year career as a journalist. In
doing so, it overlooks Addison's literary methods, such as his
use of characterised mouthpieces as satiric vehicles. Strongest
on Addison as a political writer; discussions of his moral essays
tend towards overgeneralisation.

AS5   Otten, Robert M.
JOSEPH ADDISON, Twayne *English Authors* series
(Boston: 1982)

A brief survey of Addison's prose, verse and drama, with
special emphasis on the minor works.

Periodicals

AS6   Friedman, Albert
'Addison's Ballad Papers and the Reaction to Metaphysical
Wit', *Comparative Literature* 12 (1960) 1–12 (reprinted in *The
Ballad Revival* (Chicago: 1961) 84–113)

Friedman argues that the ballad revival of the first half of the
eighteenth century was sponsored by neo-classicism rather than
reflecting a growing trend to Romanticism. He suggests that the
'ballad papers', *Spectator* Nos. 70, 74 and 85, are not self-
contained but should be read in conjunction with the essay on
true and false wit which appears in *Spectator* Nos. 58–63.
Interprets the appeal of the ballads in Addison's eyes as examples of 'classical' simplicity.

AS7   Mahoney, John L.
'Addison and Akenside: The Impact of Psychological
Criticism on Early English Romantic Poetry', *British Journal
of Aesthetics* vi (1966) 365–74

A fresh and stimulating paper taking an original approach to
Addison.

AS8 SALTER, C. H.
'Dryden and Addison', *MLR* 69 (1974) 29–39

Salter argues that many of Addison's critical comments are echoes of Dryden's established views.

References to Addison in Other Works

AS9 Lewis, C. S.
'ADDISON', ESSAYS ON THE EIGHTEENTH CENTURY PRESENTED TO DAVID NICHOL SMITH (Oxford: 1945) 1–14

Attempts to define Addison's characteristics as a writer in contrast to Pope and Swift. Portrays Addison as living at a time of great change in the history of sensibility, especially in his appreciation of ballad poetry.

AS10 Hansen, David A.
'Addison on Ornament and Poetic Style', STUDIES IN CRITICISM AND AESTHETICS 1660–1800 (ed. Howard Anderson and John S. Shea) (Minneapolis: 1967) 94–127

Discusses the role of 'ornament' in Addison's poetic theories, making a distinction between the 'straightforward' moral messages of prose writers and the poet's use of 'description, illustration, circumstance, or metaphor' to turn a didactic theme into a 'pleasant' experience. 'Addison values ornament not as an end in itself but as a means of forming the style that has the most pleasing effects'.

Steele, Richard (1672–1729)

Editions

AS11 Blanchard, Rae (ed.)
THE OCCASIONAL VERSE OF RICHARD STEELE (Oxford: 1952)

Contains a useful critical introduction and an extensive and informative commentary.

Full-length Studies

AS12   Winton, Calhoun
CAPTAIN STEELE (Baltimore: 1964); SIR RICHARD
STEELE, M.P. (Baltimore: 1970)

A two-volume biography of Steele. Winton provides a sound if
unexciting narrative work, synthesising recent scholarship but
without great claims to originality.

AS13   Dammers, Richard H.
RICHARD STEELE, Twayne *English Authors* series
(Boston: 1982)

In common with other volumes in the series, Dammers' work
provides an accessible introduction to the subject for the non-
specialist reader. A good starting-point for readers who require
a brief and lively account; with less emphasis on Steele's
political career than that provided by Winton's scholarly biography (AS12).

Addison and Steele – Works of General Interest

AS14   Humphreys, A. R.
STEELE, ADDISON AND THEIR PERIODICAL
ESSAYS, *Writers and Their Works* series (London: 1959)

A brief but entertaining introduction to Addison and Steele and
their relationship with the genre of the periodical essay. Contains a short bibliography.

AS15   Bond, Donald F.
THE SPECTATOR (Oxford: 1965), 5 vols.

A scholarly, critical edition with an extensive introduction on
the authorship, publication and circulation of the paper.
Though designed for specialist readers, those new to the subject
will find much material on Augustan poetic theories by brows-
ing through these volumes.

AS16 Bloom, Edward and Lillian (eds.)
ADDISON AND STEELE: THE CRITICAL HERITAGE
(London: 1980)

In the *Critical Heritage* series, a selection of essays reflecting the critical responses to the works of Addison and Steele, including material from the eighteenth, nineteenth and twentieth centuries. Material is divided arbitrarily into seven sections: Steele the man, the pamphleteer, the dramatist, the *Tatler*, the *Spectator*, Addison the dramatist and Addison the man and writer. Much of the material is of little interest and it stands unsupported by adequate editorial comment.

AS17 Stephens, John (ed.)
THE GUARDIAN (Lexington, Kentucky: 1982)

The first scholarly edition of the paper since 1789. Copiously annotated, and well presented. Less impressive for its literary judgement than for the informative background notes.

Akenside, Mark (1721–70)

Full-length Studies

AK1   Houpt, C. T.
MARK AKENSIDE: A BIOGRAPHICAL AND
CRITICAL STUDY (Philadelphia: 1944; New York: 1970)
Summarises critical responses to Akenside and attempts a re-
evaluation.

AK2   Marsh, Robert
FOUR DIALECTICAL THEORIES OF POETRY: AN
ASPECT OF ENGLISH NEOCLASSICAL CRITICISM
(Chicago: 1965)

Marsh discusses the poetic and aesthetic theories of Akenside,
together with Shaftesbury, Hartley and James Harris.

Periodicals

AK3   Aldridge, A.
'Akenside and Imagination', *SP* 42 (1945) 769–92

Aldridge argues that Akenside must not be grouped with poets
such as Collins as forerunners of the Romantics. Analyses
Akenside's responses to contemporary thought and offers an
interpretation of Akenside's own philosophical concepts.

AK4   Marsh, Robert
'Akenside and Addison: The Problem of Ideational Debt',
MP 59 (1961) 36–48

Attempts to solve at least part of the general problem of
Akenside's debt to Addison.

AK5 Mahoney, J. L.
'Addison and Akenside: The Impact of Psychological
Criticism on Early English Romantic Poetry', *British Journal
of Aesthetics* 6 (1966) 365–74

Mahoney argues that Akenside's knowledge of Locke was
probably gleaned from his reading of Addision. Suggests that
'Lockean' psychology prompted a new concept of poetic
theory.

AK6 Norton, John
'Addison's "The Pleasures of the Imagination"': An Exercise
in Poetics', *ECS* 3 (1970) 366–83

Norton argues that 'The Pleasures of the Imagination' was not
simply a descriptive poem or a versification of Addison; Akenside was concerned with 'the processes when the mind con-
fronts the natural world' and not with the natural world for its
own sake.

Beattie, James (1735–1803)

BE1   King, Everard H.
JAMES BEATTIE, Twayne *English Authors* series (Boston: 1977)

Examines the poetry and criticism of this neglected author in the context of the Scottish Enlightenment. Offers an interesting, if not entirely convincing, re-assessment of Beattie's poem, *The Minstrel*.

Burke, Edmund (1729–97)

Full-length Studies

BU1 Newman, Bertram
EDMUND BURKE (London: 1927)

A thorough and scholarly account of Burke's life, still a useful source.

BU2 Cobban, Alfred
EDMUND BURKE AND THE REVOLT AGAINST THE EIGHTEENTH CENTURY (London: 1929)

Subtitled 'a study of the political and social thinking of Burke, Wordsworth, Coleridge and Southey'.

BU3 Bryant, Donald Cross
EDMUND BURKE AND HIS LITERARY FRIENDS (St Louis: 1939)

Bryant looks at Burke's friendships and associations with over a hundred writers and scholars.

BU4 Copeland, T. W.
OUR EMINENT FRIEND EDMUND BURKE (New Haven: 1949; London: 1950)

A collection of six essays, covering: Boswell's portrait of Burke; aspects of Burke's personality and career; Burke's journalism; Burke's book reviews for Dodsley's *Annual Register*; Burke, Paine and Jefferson; and 'Monsieur Dupont' – notes on the French Revolution.

BU5   Boulton, James T.
       THE LANGUAGE OF POLITICS IN THE AGE OF
       WILKES AND BURKE (London: 1963)

       Boulton treats Burke as the central figure, although he also
       discusses Wilkes and Paine. He proceeds, as he says, with 'the
       eye of the literary critic', looking at Burke's writings as contri-
       butions to a public debate varying in register and rhetorical
       tone. His analysis of Burke's language is close, sometimes
       almost page-by-page. A valuable and stimulating study.

BU6   Cone, C. B.
       BURKE AND THE NATURE OF POLITICS (Lexington:
       1957; 1964), 2 vols.

       A thorough and lengthy biography of Burke. Although Cone
       includes material of interest to the non-specialist, his emphasis
       is deliberately on Burke's politics: of the 900 pages overall, only
       about sixty are concerned with Burke's literary achievements.

BU7   Stanlis, Peter J. (ed.)
       EDMUND BURKE: THE ENLIGHTENMENT AND THE
       MODERN WORLD (Detroit: 1967)

       This collection of essays is mainly concerned with political and
       historical issues, but papers by Louis Bredvold and Walter
       Love are of some interest to students of literary criticism.

BU8   Chapman, Gerald W.
       EDMUND BURKE: THE PRACTICAL IMAGINATION
       (Harvard, London: 1967)

       Chapman argues that, to appreciate Burke's writing, it is
       necessary to consider both his literary and his political abilities
       and to recognise that they are closely linked. Chapman pro-
       ceeds chronologically through Burke's major areas of concern:
       America, Ireland, constitutional reform, the French Revolu-
       tion and India. He emphasises that Burke's philosophy must
       always be read in the context of specific concerns and not
       abstracted into a system.

Chatterton, Thomas (1752–70)

Bibliography

CH1   Warren, Murray
A DESCRIPTIVE AND ANNOTATED BIBLIOGRAPHY
OF THOMAS CHATTERTON (New York, London: 1977)

A thorough bibliography of Chatterton studies up to 1977.

Full-length Studies

CH2   Ellinger, Esther Parker
THOMAS CHATTERTON, THE MARVELLOUS BOY
(Philadelphia: 1930)

Ellinger's interest in this brief study is less in the Chatterton of
the Rowley poems or the *African Eclogues* than in Chatterton
the satirist. A sketchy and loosely Freudian interpretation of
the life.

CH3   Meyerstein, E. H. W.
A LIFE OF THOMAS CHATTERTON (London: 1930)

A well-researched and scholarly book, correcting several apoc-
ryphal legends about Chatterton's life.

CH4   Nevill, John Cranstoun
THOMAS CHATTERTON (London: 1948)

A critical biography compiled from earlier studies and per-
petuating some of their errors of interpretation. For example,
Nevill believes that the 'original manuscripts' are evidence of
Chatterton's growing conviction that he could imitate medieval
script: modern scholarship believes them to have been produced to answer accusations of forgery.

CH5   Cottle, Basil
THOMAS CHATTERTON (The University, Bristol, for the
Bristol Branch of the Historical Association: 1963)

A brief assessment of Chatterton as the major voice of the
Gothic revival, escaping poverty and philistinism by the creation of a fantasised version of medieval England.

CH6   Kelly, Linda
THE MARVELLOUS BOY (London: 1972)

A popularist approach presenting Chatterton as a cult figure,
concluding with a comparison to Jimi Hendrix. Sections on
biography, the Rowley controversy, and 'the legend'. Critical
comment restricted to the use of Chatterton's suicide as a
vehicle for fantasy by the next generation of writers, especially
Keats.

CH7   Taylor, Donald S.
THOMAS CHATTERTON'S ART: EXPERIMENTS IN
IMAGINED HISTORY (Princeton: 1979)

A study of the Rowley poems, with close commentary and
location of sources including Shakespeare, Collins and the
Scriblerians; but also a reminder that Chatterton was a journalist and satirist, and a hack writer of libretti for Marylebone
Gardens.

Periodicals and Shorter Articles

CH8   Taylor, Donald S.
'Chatterton: The Problem of Rowley Chronology and Its
Implications', *PQ* xlvi (1967) 268–77

Taylor organises the Rowley material on a chronological basis
through the year which Chatterton spent working on the poems
(1768–9). He analyses both internal and external evidence, and
argues that Chatterton was increasingly seeking new audiences
and patrons.

CH9   Haywood, Ian
       'Chatterton's Plans for the Publication of the Forgery', *RES*
       n.s. 36 (1985) 58–68

       Haywood suggests that, although Chatterton's poems did not
       get into print in his short lifetime, he set about a deliberate
       campaign of publicity to promote their publication.

Cibber, Colley (1671–1757)

Full-length Studies

CI1   Habbema, D. M. E.
AN APPRECIATION OF COLLEY CIBBER (Amsterdam: 1928)

Includes chapters on Cibber's life and stage career as actor–manager. Unscholarly and unoriginal.

CI2   Senior, Francesca D. P.
THE LIFE AND TIMES OF COLLEY CIBBER (London: 1928)

A light and gossipy book about Cibber and his friends.

CI3   Barker, R. H.
MR CIBBER OF DRURY LANE (London: 1939)

Mainly useful for elucidating Cibber's long career of backstage quarrels and literary feuds.

CI4   Ashley, Leonard R. N.
COLLEY CIBBER, Twayne *English Authors* series (New York: 1965)

An attempt to popularise Cibber, which fails to provide accurate information or interpretation – consisting only of sweeping generalisations and name-dropping.

CI5   Koon, Helene
COLLEY CIBBER, A BIOGRAPHY (Lexington: 1985)

Presents Cibber as 'an actor to the core', whose charismatic stage presence cannot be recaptured by reading his plays on the page. Well researched, but too full of the magic of the theatre to be a balanced literary account.

Periodicals and Shorter Articles

CI6   Gilmore, Thomas B., jun.
'Colley Cibber's Good Nature and His Reaction to Pope's
Satire', *Papers on Language and Literature* II (1966) 361–71

Gilmore argues that Cibber's 'blithe and easy banter', a characteristic of his 'good humour', was merely a variation on the
attempts of Pope's victims to wound the satirist in return.

CI7   Potter, Lois
'Colley Cibber: The Fop as Hero', AUGUSTAN WORLDS
(ed. J. C. Hilson, M. M. B. Jones and J. R. Watson) (New
York: 1978) (A48) 153–64

Argues that Cibber himself was largely responsible for the
image of himself as a clown and fop which Pope subsequently
exploited.

Collins, William (1721–59)

Full-length Studies

CO1   Doughty, O.
       WILLIAM COLLINS, *Writers and their Work* series
       (London: 1964)

       A brief introduction to Collins for the general reader.

CO2   Sigworth, Oliver F.
       WILLIAM COLLINS, Twayne *English Authors* series (New
       York: 1965)

       Sigworth argues that Collins can only be understood in the
       context of mid-eighteenth-century English poetry, and sum-
       marises contemporary poetic theories to provide a historical
       context. A useful introduction to Collins' life and background,
       although the critical commentary is not particularly perceptive
       or helpful.

CO3   Carver, P. L.
       THE LIFE OF A POET: A BIOGRAPHICAL SKETCH
       OF COLLINS (London: 1967)

       Following his important series of articles in *Notes and Queries*
       (1939) Carver was able to trace original material in the form of
       wills, parish registers, etc. His biography corrects many errors
       made by earlier critics; it is thoroughly researched and schol-
       arly, an important source book for the study of Collins.

CO4   Wendorf, Richard
       WILLIAM COLLINS AND EIGHTEENTH-CENTURY
       ENGLISH POETRY (Minneapolis: 1981)

       Restores Collins to his contemporary context in exploring his relationship with such poets as Thomson and Akenside, rather than looking to Milton and Spenser for models or to Blake and Keats for successors. Traces the development from early eighteenth-century conventions (established by Dryden and Pope) through to greater originality and revision of texts. Wendorf challenges the theory of Collins' madness as an essential part of his poetry, and argues instead that Collins achieves poetic unity through an interest in psychology, personifying in nature human attributes and aspirations. Wendorf supports all his arguments with close textual references, yet the very process of such definition results in a narrowing of theme and imposes its own reductions.

Periodicals and Shorter Articles

CO5   McKillop, A. D.
'The Romanticism of William Collins', *SP* xx (1923) 1–16

Elements of Collins' imagery which point towards the emerging Romanticism rather than Augustan conventions, emphasise a conception of melancholy underlying the pseudo-classical commonplaces.

CO6   Garrod, Heathcote W.
'The Poetry of Collins', Warton Lecture on English Poetry for 1928, *Proceedings of the British Academy* (London: 1928); COLLINS (London: 1928)

In both the text of his lecture and its expanded version, *Collins*, Garrod offers a perceptive and lively reading of the *Odes on Several . . . Subjects*, making distinctions between the political verses and those which surround them.

CO7   Spacks, Patricia Meyer
'Collins' Imagery', *SP* lxii (1965) 719–36

Spacks notes that the question of Collins' imagery has always figured largely in critical responses to his works. She offers a close reading of selected texts to demonstrate Collins' own theories of poetic imagery, and argues that his best works are structured around 'the process of discovery through images'.

CO8   Wasserman, Earl R.
'Collins' "Ode on the Poetical Character" ', *ELH* xxxiv
(1967) 92–115

Wasserman argues that the first stanza of the *Ode* locates the
poem in the tradition which opposes Christian and secular
poetry. The first stanza, he concludes, is the key to the relationship between the second and third stanzas in this tradition of
oppositions.

CO9   Johnston, Arthur
'The Poetry of William Collins', The Warton Lecture for
1973 (London: 1973)

Collins' initial impetus to write poetry is described as stemming
from 'bookish' subjects – literary history and literary controversy. Later, Johnston suggests, the Jacobite rebellion fired his
imagination. Assesses the religious sensibility which leads Collins to seek symbolism in pictorial settings.

Major References to Collins in Other Works

CO10   Woodhouse, A. S. P.
'Collins and the Creative Imagination: A Study in the Critical
Background of His Odes (1746)', STUDIES IN ENGLISH
BY MEMBERS OF UNIVERSITY COLLEGE TORONTO
(Toronto: 1931) 59–130

Reads Collins' *Odes* in the context of early-eighteenth-century
theories of the imagination. An excellent and stimulating study.

CO11   Tillotson, Geoffrey
'Notes on Collins', ESSAYS IN CRITICISM AND
RESEARCH (Cambridge: 1942) 127–30

Looks briefly at Collins' use of personification, commenting
that 'In an age which used capitals freely, not every capitalized
abstract noun was seen by the poet as a person'. Traces parallels
between Collins' apparently distinctive diction, and earlier
translations of Ovid, Homer and Virgil.

CO12 Quintana, R.
'The Scheme of Collins' Odes', RESTORATION AND
EIGHTEENTH-CENTURY LITERATURE: ESSAYS IN
HONOR OF ALAN DUGALD McKILLOP (ed.
C. Camden) (Chicago, London: 1963) (A16) 371–81

Discusses Collins' *Odes* as deliberate attempts to embody the
themes and forms of contemporary poetic theory. 'What distinguishes Collins in this respect is that his views were so
distinctly colored by the new aesthetics – and aestheticism – of
his day.' Within the poems themselves, Quintana argues, Collins is concerned to draw attention to formal structures, so that
the 'scheme' he creates is self-consciously present, guiding the
reader's interpretation.

CO13 Woodhouse, A. S. P.
'The Poetry of Collins Reconsidered', FROM SENSIBILITY
TO ROMANTICISM (ed. F. W. Hilles and H. Bloom) (New
York: 1965) 93–117

'Collins inhabited two literary worlds,' Woodhouse argues: the
first 'a palpable continuation from the earlier part of the century
when Addison, Swift and Pope' were dominant voices; the
second 'the world of tomorrow' which is 'not very easy to
describe'. On the basis of these conventional assumptions,
Woodhouse concludes that Collins' interest in primitivism de-
fines him as a pre-Romantic, though he remained fascinated by
Augustan literature, 'its surface glamour hiding the dark under-
side of struggle and disappointment'.

Cowper, William (1731–1800)

Full-length Studies

CP1 Memes, J. S.
THE LIFE OF WILLIAM COWPER (1837; reprinted New York and London, 1972)

Characteristically Victorian, Memes' biography is of interest only as an example of mid-nineteenth-century criticism.

CP2 Wright, Thomas
THE LIFE OF WILLIAM COWPER (London: 1892; reprinted 1921)

A sturdy Victorian account of Cowper's life, still of some interest but essentially superseded by modern works.

CP3 Roy, James Alexander
COWPER AND HIS POETRY (London: 1914)

A thorough study for its time, including bibliographical details on the early critics of Cowper.

CP4 Fausset, Hugh I'Anson
WILLIAM COWPER (London: 1928)

A psychological biography of William Cowper the man; interprets the poetry as an attempt to satisfy a fundamental need of his nature, a form of religion. Argues that in *The Task* Cowper foreshadows Wordsworth. In concentrating on Cowper's psychology, Fausset draws the reader's attention to the bleaker vision often obscured by the pastoral conventions.

CP5   Cecil, Lord David
       THE STRICKEN DEER, OR THE LIFE OF COWPER
       (London: 1929; reprinted in *World's Classics* series, New
       York, 1930)

       Concentrates more on Cowper's melancholy and disease than
       on his literary achievement. Cecil argues that religion, far from
       inducing Cowper's madness, was his only consolation.

CP6   Thomas, G.
       WILLIAM COWPER AND THE EIGHTEENTH
       CENTURY (London: 1935; revised 1948)

       Thomas is at pains to defend the Evangelical religion as a cause
       for Cowper's madness, which he categorises as a 'relatively
       localised' malady, seeking to prove that it is totally separate
       from Cowper's faith. Useful on the background of the Evan-
       gelical religion, but not approaching either it or Cowper
       critically.

CP7   Hartley, Lodwick
       WILLIAM COWPER, HUMANITARIAN (Chapel Hill,
       N. Carolina: 1938)

       Hartley approaches Cowper not as the reclusive and melan-
       choly poet but as a 'citizen of the world'. His emphasis is less on
       the man than on the eighteenth-century context, especially on
       the humanitarian concerns. Hartley argues that Cowper's own
       humanitarian philosophy stemmed not from rationality but
       from Christian charity.

CP8   Nicholson, Norman
       WILLIAM COWPER (London: 1951)

       Nicholson offers a stimulating introduction to Cowper's life and
       work from the perspective of a practising poet. He argues that,
       though Cowper suffered periods of insanity, 'his poetry is
       essentially the poetry of the sane', delineating the 'ordinary,
       everyday country'. Cowper was, Nicholson suggests, 'the
       spokesman for the conscience of the middle classes'. Nic-
       holson's study is particularly stimulating in his exploration of

Cowper's cultural context, including his Evangelical background and his classical interests.

CP9   Quinlan, Maurice J.
WILLIAM COWPER: A CRITICAL LIFE (Minneapolis: 1953)

Quinlan attempts a reappraisal of Cowper's life and works, taking as his central theme Cowper's Evangelical religion – which he views as essentially a faith of intellect and debate as opposed to the growing emphasis on emotion in the Anglican tradition.

CP10   Huang, Roderick
WILLIAM COWPER: NATURE POET (Oxford: 1957)

The influence of Methodism on nature poetry, and Cowper's relation to the georgic tradition of didactive and descriptive verse.

CP11   Ryskamp, Charles
WILLIAM COWPER OF THE INNER TEMPLE, ESQ. (Cambridge: 1959)

Ryskamp does not aim to produce a definitive biography; his book is a closely researched account of Cowper's early years (to 1768), relying more on fact than on interpretation. Ryskamp's own American background occasionally leads him into naive perspectives on English life; describing the public school system, he relies on the twentieth-century accounts of Orwell and Forster. A chapter on Cowper's sexuality concludes that his physical deformity (or his belief that he was physically abnormal) 'was a delusion, and part of his mental disorder'.

CP12   Golden, Morris
IN SEARCH OF STABILITY: THE POETRY OF WILLIAM COWPER (New York: 1960)

Attempts to see all of Cowper's work as 'emanating from his personality', with a propensity to mental illness mingling with more cheerful moods. Analyses recurrent themes and images in Cowper's poetry 'without concern for their aesthetic significance but rather in an effort to discover their psychological importance to Cowper'. Chapters are thus concerned with the relationships between 'Freedom and Restraint', 'Solitude and Society' and 'Stability', concluding with a detailed reading of *The Task*. In Golden's view, Cowper's poetry is at its best when it 'reflects most strongly the emotional currents in which his mind was constantly bathed', and his satirical verses were merely undertaken 'primarily as moral and mental exercizes, as time-spending therapy'.

CP13 Free, William N.
WILLIAM COWPER (New York: 1970)

A beginner's guide to Cowper, providing basic biographical information followed by a close analysis of *The Task*, and a survey of the satires, lyrics and hymns. An excellent starting point for the reader new to Cowper.

CP14 Newey, Vincent
COWPER'S POETRY: A CRITICAL STUDY AND REASSESSMENT (Liverpool: 1982)

Newey offers a confident and intelligent study of Cowper's poetry, arguing that he is 'a poet broadly of the first order'. Opening chapters offer a summary of Cowper criticism, and there are interesting points on the *Moral Satires* and *Retirement*. But the book's main strength is its detailed analysis of *The Task*, concentrating on the interdependence of religion and nature in the poem. Newey assesses Cowper as a forerunner of the Romantic poets, avoiding over-biographical reading of the texts while explicitly rejecting post-structuralist techniques.

CP15 Hutchings, Bill
THE POETRY OF WILLIAM COWPER (London: 1983)

Hutchings emphasises the formal element of the invocational style of Cowper's poetry, rather than interpreting it as a personal spiritual crisis. He points to the influence of Prior and Churchill. A general introduction to Cowper with a sound emphasis on the poetic tradition.

CP16   Priestman, Martin
COWPER'S 'TASK': STRUCTURE AND INFLUENCE
(Cambridge: 1983)

A book-by-book study of *The Task*, treating the poem as
largely self-contained, although also assessing its parallels with
The Prelude and implying a historical influence.

CP17   King, James
WILLIAM COWPER: A BIOGRAPHY (Durham,
N. Carolina: 1986)

Includes a mass of manuscript material not used by previous
biographers. A 'literary biography' which attempts to show the
connections between Cowper's life and writings.

Periodicals

CP18   Hartley, Lodwick
'Cowper and the Evangelicals: Notes on Early Biographical
Interpretations', *PMLA* lxv (1950) 719–31

The beginnings of the biographical controversy on the role of
religion in Cowper's 'madness'.

CP19   Danchin, Pierre
'William Cowper's Poetic Purpose as Seen in His Letters',
English Studies xlvi (1965) 235–44

A reading of Cowper's correspondence to cast light on his
aesthetic theory.

CP20   Gregory, Hoosag K.
'Cowper's Love of Subhuman Nature: A Psychoanalytic
Approach', *PQ* xlvi (1967) 42–57

Gregory argues that Cowper's identification with the natural
world was a psychological device allowing him to escape from
the pressures of man. His role of protector towards plants and
animals is also interpreted as allowing him to identify with God.

CP21 Boyd, David
'Satire and Pastoral in *The Task*', *Papers on Language and Literature* 10 (1974) 363–77

Comments on the nature of Cowper's satire, focusing on the themes of action, retirement and self-defence.

CP22 Trickett, Rachel
'Cowper, Wordsworth, and the Animal Fable', *RES* n.s. xxxiv (1983) 471–80

Notes Cowper's habit of writing from his own observations of nature, and the psychological purpose of his writing as a therapy for personal despair.

References to Cowper in Other Works

CP23 Deane, C. V.
ASPECTS OF EIGHTEENTH-CENTURY NATURE POETRY (Oxford: 1935) (A72) 95–9

Cowper's visual imagination compared with Thomson's *The Seasons*.

CP24 Brown, Wallace Cable
THE TRIUMPH OF FORM: A STUDY OF THE LATER MASTERS OF THE HEROIC COUPLET (Chapel Hill, N. Carolina: 1948) (A74) 132–41

Cowper's heroic couplet seen as freer than that of Pope and Johnson. Poetry in the neo-classical tradition, yet criticism anticipating Keats.

CP25 Bernbaum, Ernest
GUIDE THROUGH THE ROMANTIC MOVEMENT (New York: 1949) 22–3

Cowper as a charming, sentimental pre-Romantic.

CP26   Bishop, Morchard
       BLAKE'S HAYLEY: THE LIFE, WORKS AND
       FRIENDSHIPS OF WILLIAM HAYLEY (London: 1951)

       Valuable discussion of the final decade of Cowper's life. Also
       describes Hayley's biography of Cowper.

Crabbe, George (1754–1832)

Bibliography

CR1   Bareham, T. and S. Gatrell
A BIBLIOGRAPHY OF GEORGE CRABBE (Hamden,
Connecticut: 1979)

Full-length Studies

CR2   Evans, J. H.
THE POEMS OF CRABBE: A LITERARY AND
HISTORICAL STUDY (London: 1933)

Evans offers an imaginative attempt to link Crabbe's verse
descriptions with his various clerical incumbencies; but not a
serious approach to Crabbe.

CR3   Haddakin, Lilian
THE POETRY OF CRABBE (London: 1955)

Haddakin argues that, although of limited range, Crabbe's
poetry is entitled to serious consideration.

CR4   Brett, R. L.
CRABBE, *Writers and their Works* series (1956 British
Council pamphlet)

Brett summarises the common critical views of Crabbe and
argues convincingly against them.

CR5   Chamberlain, R. L.
CRABBE (New York: 1965)

A lively account of the man and his works, approaching the
subject sympathetically. Includes a brief bibliography.

CR6   Sigworth, O. F.
NATURE'S STERNEST PAINTER: FIVE ESSAYS ON
THE POETRY OF CRABBE (Tucson, Arizona: 1965)

The five essays each deal with a different aspect of Crabbe's
poetry: the eighteenth-century milieu; his links with the Romantic movement; his nature poetry; his narrative poetry; and
criticism. Lacking in an overall interpretation of his works.

CR7   Pollard, Arthur (ed.)
CRABBE: THE CRITICAL HERITAGE (London: 1972)

In the *Critical Heritage* series, reprinting contemporary critics
on Crabbe; wide-ranging, but short on editorial control of
textual reading.

CR8   Lewis, C. Day
CRABBE (London: 1973)

Lewis argues that in Crabbe's poetry 'we have to look for the
subtle variations of an apparently monotonous surface'. The
quiet tone of Crabbe's poetry is, Lewis suggests, a counterpart
to his melodramatic plots.

CR9   Hatch, Ronald, B.
CRABBE'S ARABESQUE: SOCIAL DRAMA IN THE
POETRY OF GEORGE CRABBE (Montreal, London:
1976)

Hatch explores the conflict of ideas, especially within social
philosophies, as embodied in the characters of Crabbe's narrative poems.

CR10   Nelson, Beth
GEORGE CRABBE AND THE PROGRESS OF
EIGHTEENTH CENTURY NARRATIVE VERSE
(Lewisburg, Pennsylvania: 1976)

The literary background to Crabbe's poetry; patterns of verse-
narrative as the starting-point of his poems.

CR11 New, Peter
GEORGE CRABBE'S POETRY (London: 1976)

Starting from Leavis's comment that Crabbe was 'hardly at the fine point of consciousness in his time', New presents the fashionable aspects of his life – as an Anglican clergyman, socially distant from the younger generation of university-bred Romantics, such as Coleridge and Wordsworth. Comparing Crabbe to Wordsworth, New suggests that the latter's gain in originality may also be a loss of social context for poetic sensibility.

CR12 Bareham, Terence
GEORGE CRABBE (New York: 1977)

Bareham argues that, rather than the 'last Augustan', Crabbe was a 'Regency' poet, intensely aware of the social and cultural context of the period 1780–1830. Rather than a complex poet, Bareham sees Crabbe as an Anglican preacher concerned with morally orthodox intentions.

Periodicals

CR13 Sale, A.
'Chaucer in Cancer', *English* 6 (Summer 1947) 240–4

Sale offers a stimulating comparison of Crabbe with Chaucer.

CR14 Sale, A.
'The Development of Crabbe's Narrative Art', *Cambridge Journal* 5 (May 1952) 480–98

Argues for Crabbe's high status as a narrative poet, tracing the development of his narrative techniques.

CR15 Broman, W. E.
'Factors in Crabbe's Eminence in the Early Nineteenth Century', *MP* 51 (August 1953) 42–9

Broman argues that contemporary critical esteem for Crabbe was based on an unrepresentative poem, *The Village*.

CR16   Thale, R. M.
'Crabbe's "Village" and Topographical Poetry', *JEGP* 55
(1956) 618–23

Thale argues that the structure of *The Village* is to be understood in the context of popular topographical poetry.

CR17   Speirs, John
'Crabbe as Master of the Verse Tale', *Oxford Review* I
(1966) 3–40

Speirs sees Crabbe as 'one of the great English provincials'; yet,
he argues, Crabbe also inherits the role of urbane moral
observer from Pope and Johnson.

CR18   Diffey, Carole T.
'Journey to Experience: Crabbe's "Selford Hall" ', *Durham
University Journal* n.s. xxx (1969) 129–34

Diffey reads Crabbe's *Selford Hall* as a quest from innocence to
experience.

CR19   Brewster, Elizabeth
'George Crabbe and William Wordsworth', *University of

Toronto Quarterly* 42 (1973) 142–56

A discussion of the similarities between Crabbe and Wordsworth, and of the strains in their relationship.

References to Crabbe in Other Works

CR20   Heath-Stubbes, J.
'Crabbe and the Eighteenth Century', PENGUIN NEW
WRITING, vol. 25 (1945) 129–45

Approaches Crabbe as an Augustan poet despite the contemporary Romantic movement; but his concern with psychological states links the two traditions.

CR21 Brown, W. C.
THE TRIUMPH OF FORM (Chapel Hill, N. Carolina:
1948) (A74)

Brown notes that *Tales of the Hall* uses the heroic couplet for
narrative purposes, continuing Dryden's tradition.

CR22 Ker, W. P.
ON MODERN LITERATURE (London: 1955) 62–77

Ker argues that Crabbe's 'unpoetic' style is admirably suited to
his narrative themes.

CR23 Hodgart, P. and T. Redpath
ROMANTIC PERSPECTIVES: THE WORK OF
CRABBE, BLAKE, WORDSWORTH AND
COLERIDGE AS SEEN BY THEIR
CONTEMPORARIES AND THEMSELVES (London:
1964)

Contains many of the famous critical articles on Crabbe, and
also a valuable introductory essay providing a context for
understanding the status of the reviews.

CR24 Hibbard, G. R.
'Crabbe and Shakespeare', RENAISSANCE AND
MODERN ESSAYS (ed. G. R. Hibbard) (London: 1966)
83–93

'Regarding the heroic as the highest form of poetry, the great
Augustans had more sense than to write it'. Hibbard argues
that, by contrast, the Romantics were foolish enough to write
Shakespearean imitations, producing 'a series of miscarriages,
still births and monsters'. Between these two extremes he
locates the poetry of Crabbe, whom he sees as adapting Elizabethan material successfully according to the tastes of his own
age: 'something of Shakespeare's attitude, and especially of his
humanity, passes into his own work with a broadening and
fertilizing effect'.

CR25   Hayter, A.
OPIUM AND THE ROMANTIC IMAGINATION
(London: 1968) 165–90

Hayter discusses the effects of opium on Crabbe's poetic
creativity; a full and useful exploration.

CR26   Thomas, W. K.
'George Crabbe: Not Quite the Sternest', STUDIES IN
ROMANTICISM vii (1968) 166–75

Thomas challenges the reading of Crabbe as 'nature's sternest
painter'. He also argues that Crabbe was not an original poet,
but was heavily indebted to John Langhorne.

CR27   Abrams, Meyer H.
THE MILK OF PARADISE (New York: 1970)

The effect of opium visions on the works of De Quincey,
Crabbe, Francis Thompson and Coleridge.

CR28   Burden, D. H.
'Crabbe and the Augustan Tradition', ESSAYS AND

POEMS PRESENTED TO LORD DAVID CECIL (ed.
W. W. Robson) (London: 1970) 77-92

Burden argues that Crabbe's realism is the result of experience
filtered through 'clerical habituation'. Working within an established literary tradition, Crabbe still created an individual style.
Although he claimed that poetry deserved a wider province
through his work, the role of poetry was being taken over by the
novel.

Denham, John (1615–69)

Full-length Studies

DE1   Banks, Howard Theodore
        THE POETICAL WORKS OF SIR JOHN DENHAM
        (London: 1928; reprinted 1969)

        Banks' work has now been superseded by that of O Hehir
        (DE2). The critical commentary included in Banks' volume
        should not be relied upon as it is outdated and inaccurate.

DE2   O Hehir, Brendan
        HARMONY FROM DISCORDS: A LIFE OF SIR JOHN
        DENHAM (Berkeley, Los Angeles: 1969)

        O Hehir provides a substantial and well-researched biography
        of Denham, incorporating much detailed information and cor-
        recting misinterpretations which have been handed down as
        'facts'. The first half of the book concentrates on the main
        events of Denham's life up to the Restoration – Strafford's trial
        in 1641, and Denham's exile in the early 1650s for loyalty to the
        Royalist cause. O Hehir demonstrates the importance of these
        events for an understanding of *Coopers Hill*, and goes on to
        suggest that they are the key to Denham's personality. For his
        life after 1660, O Hehir identifies the main event as his tempo-
        rary insanity in 1666, which he reads as a form of psychological
        collapse brought on by personal failure and an unhappy mar-
        riage. O Hehir's biography is meticulously thorough and histor-
        ically accurate, an invaluable source for students of Denham.

Periodicals

DE3   Korshin, Paul J.
        'The Evolution of Neoclassical Poetics: Cleveland, Denham
        and Waller as Poetic Theorists', *ECS* II (1968) 102–37

'The transition from metaphysical to neoclassical English poetry involves the rejection of one set of theoretical assumptions
about the intentions and methods of poetry and the acceptance
in its place of a new poetics which its practitioners firmly
believed to be better than the old'. Korshin argues that the
transition from seventeenth- to eighteenth-century poetry was
a deliberate process influenced by 'linguistic theories, the
growth of scientific utilitarianism, and the slow influence of
toleration upon the religion and political divisions of the first
half of the century'.

DE4   Wallace, John M.
'*Coopers Hill*: The Manifesto of Parliamentary Royalism,
1641', *ELH* 41 (1974) 494–540

Wallace analyses the topographical poem in the political context of 1641, suggesting that it was probably written in Septem-
ber of that year. He suggests that the symbol of the stag, rather
than being a specific reference to Strafford, should be read as a
general symbol of arbitrary power.

References to Denham in Other Works

DE5   Cohen, Ralph
'Innovation and Variation: Literary Change and Georgic
Poetry', LITERATURE AND HISTORY (ed. R. Cohen
and M. Krieger) (Los Angeles: 1974)

Cohen argues that Denham extends the range of georgic poetry
by his 'concrete dimension of place'.

Dryden, John (1631–1700)

Bibliographies and Editions

DR1   Zamonski, John A.
AN ANNOTATED BIBLIOGRAPHY OF JOHN
DRYDEN: TEXTS AND STUDIES, 1949–73 (New York,
London: 1975)

DR2   Latt, David J. and Samuel Holt Monk
JOHN DRYDEN: A SURVEY AND BIBLIOGRAPHY
OF CRITICAL STUDIES, 1895–1974 (Minneapolis: 1976)

DR3   Swedenberg, H. T. (gen. ed.)
THE WORKS OF JOHN DRYDEN (Berkeley, Los
Angeles: 1956–)

This, the 'California Dryden', is the definitive edition. Still in
progress, it is projected to fill twenty volumes. With full scholarly apparatus and useful critical introductions by leading
commentators on Dryden.

Full-length Studies

DR4   Saintsbury, George
DRYDEN, *English Men of Letters* (London: 1902)

The chief difficulty in writing a life of Dryden, Saintsbury
observes, is the 'almost entire absence of materials'. He deals
with this difficulty well, offering a lively impressionistic study
full of firm opinions and colourful anecdotes much in the
manner of the period. He concludes: 'the eighteen volumes of
his works contain a faithful representation of the whole literary
movement in England for the best part of half a century, and
what is more, they contain the germs and indicate the direction
of almost the whole literary movement for nearly a century
more'.

DR5   Van Doren, Mark
JOHN DRYDEN (New York: 1920; Cambridge: 1931)

An informal if predictable portrait, rehashing several familiar
attitudes to Dryden. Van Doren presents him as 'a journalist in
verse', a man 'without conspicuous principles of his own concerning church or state', for whom 'style was paramount'.

DR6   Eliot, T. S.
JOHN DRYDEN, THE POET, THE DRAMATIST, THE
CRITIC (New York: 1932)

Eliot concentrates upon, and celebrates, Dryden's status and
influence in a defined literary tradition. 'Being so completely
representative, Dryden not only formed the mould for the next
age, but himself derived very clearly from the last'. Full of
cavalier historical generalisations and literary assertions,
mingled with some perceptive comments on Dryden's plays and
criticism.

DR7   Bredvold, L. I.
THE INTELLECTUAL MILIEU OF JOHN DRYDEN
(Ann Arbor, Michigan: 1934)

In its time Bredvold's study represented an important break-
through both in the critical appreciation of Dryden and in the
area of contextual analysis. His presentation of Dryden's intellectual milieu centres on the concept of philosophical scepticism. Dryden's ideological hesitancy – sometimes called
opportunism – is described by Bredvold as 'something more
positive than indecision; it is less a weakness of will than a
richness and suppleness of intellect'. In this way, Bredvold
argues, Dryden's wit captures the essential quality of 'an age of
philosophical scepticism . . . Neither Dryden nor his age can be
fully understood apart from this Pyrrhonism, diffused in every
department of thought'. Often subtle and persuasive, Bredvold's thesis is over-schematic and his interpretation of Dryden's intellectual milieu has been significantly challenged by
Harth (DR25) and Fujimura (DR42).

DR8 Allen, Ned Bliss
THE SOURCES OF JOHN DRYDEN'S COMEDIES
University of Michigan Publications, *Language and
Literature*, vol. xvi (Ann Arbor, Michigan: 1935)

A scholarly thesis, of interest to the specialist only.

DR9 Osborn, James M.
JOHN DRYDEN: SOME BIOGRAPHICAL FACTS AND
PROBLEMS (New York: 1940)

Rather than offering a full-dress biography, Osborn does some
'preliminary digging' to ensure that any future biography might
be based on firm factual foundations. His careful, methodical
researches through earlier memoirs, anecdotes and biographies
of Dryden are fascinating as he sifts fact from fiction, truth from
legend. Whereas Saintsbury (DR4) had complained of an
'almost entire absence of materials', Osborn unearthed solid
materials which eventually assisted Charles Ward in writing his
biography (DR15).

DR10 Smith, David Nichol
JOHN DRYDEN (the Clark Lectures on English Literature,
1948–9) (London, New York: 1950)

Four lectures on Dryden: early verse and criticism; plays;
satires and religious poems; and translations, odes and
fables.

DR11 Fujimura, T. H.
THE RESTORATION COMEDY OF WIT (Princeton:
1952)

Drawing many examples from Dryden's plays and criticism,
Fujimura attempts to demonstrate the difference between
'intrinsic' and 'peripheral' meanings in the comedies of the
period.

DR12   Young, Kenneth
JOHN DRYDEN, A CRITICAL BIOGRAPHY (London: 1954)

'Writing a life of John Dryden is like trying to carve in solid rock with a tablespoon', says Young. His own chosen tablespoon is psychoanalysis, which yields some interesting speculations.

DR13   Frost, William
DRYDEN AND THE ART OF TRANSLATION (New Haven: 1955)

Only recently, in such studies as those by David Hopkins (DR37) and Emrys Jones (A64), have Dryden's translations come to receive the critical attention they merit. Frost's brief and self-confessedly 'exploratory' study is as much concerned with quantity as quality. 'In sheer bulk, the translations make up approximately two thirds of all his poetry'. The analysis is disappointing, moving from generalisations about theories of translation to technical discussions of Dryden's vocabulary. Some interesting detailed discussion of selected passages from Chaucer and Virgil.

DR14   Schilling, Bernard N.
DRYDEN AND THE CONSERVATIVE MYTH: A READING OF *ABSALOM AND ACHITOPHEL* (New Haven: 1961)

This book examines Dryden's poem in the context of the established iconography of what Schilling calls 'conservative myth'. He describes Dryden as 'the classical figure of literary conservatism'. The book falls into two halves: the first, historical and scholarly, traces the emergence of the 'conservative myth' in English political thought during the seventeenth century; the second, which is analytical and critical, discusses key images of architecture, disease and madness. Though sometimes in danger of losing sight of the poetry amid all the political codes, the book is lucid and accurate.

DR15 Ward, Charles E.
THE LIFE OF JOHN DRYDEN (Chapel Hill, N. Carolina; London: 1961)

Prolific as a writer, John Dryden remains elusive as a personality; and this book, while avoiding speculative theories, offers a convincing portrait of man and works. It is particularly good on the political writings, examining Dryden's 'epic dream' of celebrating the Stuart dynasty and offering a new interpretation of *Annus Mirabilis*. Ward chooses 'to exclude critical pronouncement'. The information and interpretations which he presents in this synthesis of recent scholarship allows critical exploration of Dryden's poetry to proceed on a sound basis of fact.

DR16 Hoffman, Arthur W.
JOHN DRYDEN'S IMAGERY (Gainsville, Florida: 1962)

Through an analysis of recurrent images Hoffman discusses the significance of metaphor and simile in the structure and meaning of Dryden's poetry. Hoffman identifies three key sets of images: theological, political and literary, though the three categories frequently intermix. He sees Dryden's chief poetic achievement in the combination of traditional images drawn from biblical or classical sources with contemporary images of food, sex and commerce.

DR17 Aden, John M.
THE CRITICAL OPINIONS OF JOHN DRYDEN: A DICTIONARY (Nashville: 1963)

Aden has compiled and edited this dictionary of Dryden's critical opinions, taking his entries from the whole of the prose works including essays, prefaces, notes, histories and letters. Entries run from 'Academy' to 'Youth', with some of the longest entries being, predictably, on 'Satire' and 'Tragedy'.

DR18 Schilling, Bernard (ed.)
DRYDEN: A COLLECTION OF CRITICAL ESSAYS, *Twentieth Century Views* (Englewood Cliffs: 1963)

A useful and representative collection of essays.

DR19   Wasserman, George R.
JOHN DRYDEN, Twayne *English Authors* series (New
York: 1964)

A useful critical study of Dryden's life and works.

DR20   Kirsch, Arthur C.
DRYDEN'S HEROIC DRAMA (Princeton, New Jersey:
1965)

Kirsch examines both the theory and practice of heroic drama,
analysing Dryden's plays not only in the light of his own critical
axioms but in comparison with the works of other neo-classical
dramatists, such as Corneille. He argues that *Aureng-Zebe*
'marks a profound change of direction in Dryden's practice – a
change away from the Cornelian celebration of *gloire* to a
growing sentimentalism'.

DR21   Roper, Alan
DRYDEN'S POETIC KINGDOMS (London: 1965)

An interesting attempt to recapture the imaginative force and
function (rather than the historical meaning) of Dryden's poetic
allusions. History becomes part of poetry rather than verse
serving to sweeten propaganda. Some useful passages of close
analysis.

DR22   Swedenberg, H. T. (ed.)
ESSENTIAL ARTICLES FOR THE STUDY OF JOHN
DRYDEN (London: 1966)

A valuable collection of reprinted essays in the 'Essential
Articles' series. Contains, among other notable contributions,
James Kinsley's 'Dryden and the Art of Praise'.

DR23   Miner, Earl
DRYDEN'S POETRY (Bloomington, Indiana, London:
1967)

Favouring a selective rather than a comprehensive approach,
Miner examines a representative sample of Dryden's works and
distinguishes certain key concepts. Harmony is one of these – 'a

word which appears repeatedly in his poetry, and is itself an apt conception of the character of his poetry at its best' (p. 289). Harmony and order are presented as a natural preoccupation for a poet who had lived through the political turmoil of the mid seventeenth century. Miner examines similarities and differences between the poetry of Dryden and Donne. After Dryden's conversion to Catholicism, Miner finds him returning to a use of conceits and 'to a kind of private allusive style' more richly metaphysical even than *Absalom and Achitophel.*

DR24   Davison, Dennis
        DRYDEN, *Literature in Perspective* series (London: 1968)

        Analyses the poems in context. Davison describes Dryden's 'rococo finery' as having 'a steel framework of earnest concern for man and society'.

DR25   Harth, Philip
        CONTEXTS OF DRYDEN'S THOUGHT (Chicago: 1968)

        An important book which challenges the orthodox assumptions about Dryden's intellectual environment established by Bredvold's *Intellectual Milieu of John Dryden* (1934) (DR7). The first two chapters distinguish between Dryden's scepticism in matters of art and science and his dogmatism concerning religion and politics. Four chapters are devoted to *Religio Laici*, commentating on Dryden's rejection of Deism. The last two chapters are devoted to *The Hind and the Panther*. Harth concludes that while Dryden is entirely Anglican in *Religio Laici* and entirely Catholic in *The Hind and the Panther*, he is philosophically moderate in both poems.

DR26   Ramsey, Paul
        THE ART OF JOHN DRYDEN (Lexington, Kentucky: 1969)

        From a reading of Dryden's critical essays, Ramsey identifies two principal ideals of poetry: harmony and propriety. He proceeds from this to a discussion of the versification and structure of Dryden's poetry. His study moves from technical analysis of poetic devices to a critical appreciation of poetic strengths.

DR27   King, Bruce (ed.)
DRYDEN'S MIND AND ART (Edinburgh: 1969; New
York: 1970)

A collection of essays of various periods and authorships. In his
own essay King sees *Absalom and Achitophel* as an 'anatomy'
satirising a cast of mind.

DR28   Kinsley, James and Helen (eds.)
DRYDEN: THE CRITICAL HERITAGE (New York,
London: 1971)

A selection of criticisms from 1660 to 1810.

DR29   Miner, Earl (ed.)
JOHN DRYDEN, *Writers and Their Background*
(Athens, Ohio, London: 1972)

Includes bibliography. All new articles: Miner's contribution
explores Dryden's reputation, works and literary milieu.

DR30   Myers, William
DRYDEN (London: 1973)

A book which damns with faint praise. Myers accepts that
Dryden's metaphors of kingship are 'without interest, either
psychologically or politically'. He also presents Dryden
'trapped inside neo-classical notions of responsibility, which
severely limited his freedom to use what words and portray
what characters he chose'. Myers sets out to show 'how im-
pressively he in fact learned to deploy a limited and perhaps
debased poetic idiom' but the attempt is timid and
unconvincing.

DR31   Garrison, James D.
DRYDEN AND THE TRADITION OF PANEGYRIC
(Berkeley, Los Angeles, London: 1975)

Essentially a taxonomic exercise seeking to define and dis-
tinguish meanings of panegyric, verse-panegyric, rhetoric and
oratory.

DR32 Pechter, Edward
DRYDEN'S CLASSICAL THEORY OF LITERATURE
(New York, London, Cambridge: 1975)

Pechter sees the structure of Dryden's critical theory as consisting in 'doubleness' and of his classicism in 'the golden mean'.
His ideas are unoriginal but sensible.

DR33 McFadden, George
DRYDEN, THE PUBLIC WRITER 1660–85 (Princeton:
1978)

Offered as a supplement to Charles Ward's 'indispensable'
biography (DR15), McFadden's book shows how Dryden used
his poetic gifts 'to put the life of his time before the imagination
of his contemporaries'. Strongly emphasises the public context
of both Dryden's poetry and his personality. In a careful and
fascinating exploration of Dryden's relations with Sir Robert
Howard he provides a model of contextual literary analysis.
Also strong on 'Dryden among the Courtiers' and *Absalom and
Achitophel.*

DR34 Atkins, G. Douglas
THE FAITH OF JOHN DRYDEN: CHANGE AND
CONTINUITY (Lexington, Kentucky: 1980)

An account of 'Dryden's religious positions from beginning to
end', this is in fact less a study of Dryden's 'faith' than of his
'anti-clericism'. He describes Dryden's family as 'fanatics' who
are 'flaming and bigoted'.

DR35 Hughes, Derek
DRYDEN'S HEROIC PLAYS (London: 1981)

Dryden's heroic plays, asserts Hughes, are 'humane, intelligent
and subtle studies of the disparity between Herculean aspiration and human reality'. A conscientious blow-by-blow study of
these neglected plays, which introduces occasional shafts of
insight into routine critical commentary.

DR36   Zwicker, Steven N.
POLITICS AND LANGUAGE IN DRYDEN'S POETRY
(Princeton: 1984)

Beginning with a chapter on 'language as disguise', Zwicker's
thoughtful volume approaches Dryden's poetry via the charged
language of political controversy and debate in late-seven-
teenth-century England. This study of the art of political lying
paves the way for studies of Dryden's ambiguities and uncer-
tainties, tropes and strategies. Zwicker offers some excellent
insights into the combined effects of classical and contemporary
allusions in Dryden's vocabulary. A very useful book.

DR37   Hopkins, David
JOHN DRYDEN (Cambridge: 1986)

A spirited celebration of Dryden's imaginative vitality.
Hopkins rejects the conventional critical concentration on
Dryden's satires, presenting him instead as a 'late developer'
whose best work is to be found in the translations.

DR38   Winn, James A.
JOHN DRYDEN AND HIS WORLD (New Haven,
London: 1987)

The chief quality of this excellent biography lies in Winn's
detailed unravelling of the complex skein of personal and
political allusions contained in Dryden's poetry. Carefully analysing the twists and turns of Dryden's career, Winn discerns a
consistent ecumenical irony underlying the variable sentiments
of the public rhetoric. Meticulously researched, this book is full
of illuminating insights and informative detail.

Periodicals and Shorter Articles

DR39   Arnold, Matthew
Introduction to *The English Poets* (1880), reprinted as 'The
Study of Poetry' in ESSAYS IN CRITICISM, second series
(1888)

See under Pope (P68).

DR40 Eliot, T. S.
'Homage to John Dryden' (London: 1924)

A spirited defence of Dryden's poetry in a review of Van Doren's book (DR5).

DR41 Dobree, Bonamy
'John Dryden', WRITERS AND THEIR WORK, 70 (New York, London: 1956)

An affectionate and unstrenuous tribute which concludes by celebrating Dryden as 'the superb all-round man'.

DR42 Fujimura, Thomas H.
'Dryden's *Religio Laici*: An Anglican Poem', *PMLA* lxxvi (1961) 205–17

An important challenge to Bredvold's analysis (DR7) of Dryden's intellectual and religious development. Fujimura argues that, far from demonstrating Roman Catholic tendencies, *Religio Laici* is an Anglican poem constituting an important contribution to Anglican apologetics.

DR43 Hart, Jeffrey
'John Dryden: The Politics of Style', *Modern Age* viii (1964) 399–408

Hart argues that the poet's 'subordination of metaphor and conceit' reveals attitudes 'that go beyond the writing of verse, and that involve the deepest questions of politics and morals'.

DR44 Wallace, John M.
'Dryden and History: A Problem in Allegorical Reading', *ELH* xxxvi (1969) 265–90

An interesting article which argues that modern critics are too cautious in interpreting the historical element in Dryden's verse. By seizing on specific 'allegories' we may ignore the broader satiric game of extrapolating wider historical parallels.

DR45   Frost, William
'Dryden and Satire', *SEL* xi (1971) 401–16

Studies Dryden's precise usage and understanding of the term
'satire'.

DR46   Harth, Phillip
'Legends No Histories: The Case of *Absalom and
Achitophel*', STUDIES IN EIGHTEENTH-CENTURY
CULTURE, vol. 4 (Madison, Wisconsin: 1975)

Harth argues that chronology proves *Absalom and Achitophel*
was not a 'cowardly attack' on Shaftesbury, or a mere piece of
government propaganda designed to influence his trial. It had a
larger purpose 'to affect public attitudes towards past events
and current policy'.

Major References to Dryden in Other Works

DR47   Highet, Gilbert
THE CLASSICAL TRADITION: GREEK AND ROMAN
INFLUENCES ON WESTERN LITERATURE (Oxford:
1949)

Various notes on Dryden's poems setting them in the context of
their classical backgrounds.

DR48   Jack, Ian
AUGUSTAN SATIRE (Oxford: 1952) (A7)

Interesting chapters on *MacFlecknoe* and *Absalom and
Achitophel*.

DR49   Leyburn, Ellen Douglas
SATIRIC ALLEGORY: MIRROR OF MAN, *York Studies
in English* 130 (New Haven: 1956)

Concentrates on *Absalom and Achitophel* and *MacFlecknoe*,
placing Dryden's use of allegory in a tradition from Erasmus to
the twentieth century.

DR50 Lees, F. N.
'John Dryden', THE PELICAN GUIDE TO ENGLISH
LITERATURE (ed. Boris Ford), vol. IV (London: 1957)

DR51 Williamson, George
THE PROPER WIT OF POETRY (Chicago, London,
Toronto: 1961)

Discusses Dryden's response to the problems posed by his
poetic predecessors: 'the regulation of wit' (pp. 84–134).

DR52 Brower, Reuben A.
'Dryden and the "Invention" of Pope', RESTORATION
AND EIGHTEENTH-CENTURY LITERATURE:
ESSAYS IN HONOUR OF ALAN DUGALD McKILLOP
(Chicago, London: 1963) 211–33

Discusses Dryden's Horatian style and its personal, colloquial
tone.

DR53 Barnes, T. R.
ENGLISH VERSE: VOICE AND MOVEMENT FROM
WYATT TO YEATS (Cambridge: 1967)

Studies the 'sounds' of poetic verse; many references to
Dryden.

DR54 Meadows, A. J.
THE HIGH FIRMAMENT: A STUDY OF ASTRONOMY
IN ENGLISH LITERATURE (Leicester: 1969)

Scattered notes on Dryden's use of astrology.

DR55 Sutherland, James R.
ENGLISH LITERATURE IN THE LATE
SEVENTEENTH CENTURY (New York, Oxford: 1969)

Comprehensive essays on Dryden.

DR56   Knights, L. C.
'Public Voices: Literature and Politics with Special Reference to the Seventeenth Century', Clark Lectures for 1970–1 (London: 1971)

Describes Dryden as a 'simplifier', tending towards abstractions which are then 'obfuscated by his rhetoric'.

Dyer, John (1699–1758)

DY1   Humfrey, Belinda
      JOHN DYER (Cardiff: 1980)

An intelligent and sympathetic approach to Dyer, consisting of a brief biography and critical study. Humfrey's interpretations of the less complex poems, such as *A Country Walk*, show a good appreciation of Dyer's attitudes to landscape. In her discussion of the later poems, however, the lack of space results in a compression and over-simplification of material, and her criticisms lack detail.

Finch, Anne (Countess of Winchilsea) (1661–1720)

Periodical

F1   Brower, Reuben A.
      'Lady Winchilsea and the Poetic Tradition of the Seventeenth
      Century', *SP* 42 (1945) 61–80

      'The majority of her poems exhibit one or more typically
      Augustan qualities: the characteristic neatness and plainness of
      verse structure, the social and aristocratic tone, the religious
      solemnity and high morality, and the inevitable fondness for the
      satirical attitude'.

References to Finch in Other Works

F2   Buxton, J.
      'The Poems of the Countess of Winchilsea', A TRADITION
      OF POETRY (London: 1967) (A83)

F3   Rogers, Katherine M.
      FEMINISM IN EIGHTEENTH-CENTURY ENGLAND
      (Brighton: 1982) (A54)

      Informative references to Finch, including a biographical sum-
      mary and interpretative comments on Finch's decision to circu-
      late her poems in manuscript rather than publication.

Garrick, David (1717–79)

GAR1 Hainsworth, J. D.
DAVID GARRICK, SELECTED VERSE, *University of New England Monographs* 2 (Armidale, Australia: 1981)

Now mainly if not exclusively known for his theatrical talents, Garrick was also a competent minor poet. Hainsworth emphasises the conversational qualities of Garrick's occasional epigrams and satires.

Gay, John (1685–1732)

Bibliographies and Editions

G1   Klein, Julie Thompson
      JOHN GAY, AN ANNOTATED CHECKLIST OF
      CRITICISM (Troy, New York: 1974)

G2   Dearing, Vinton A. and C. E. Beckwith (eds.)
      JOHN GAY, POETRY AND PROSE (Oxford: 1974),
      2 vols.

G3   Fuller, John (ed.)
      JOHN GAY, DRAMATIC WORKS (Oxford: 1983), 2 vols.

Full-length Studies

G4   Schutz, William Eben
      GAY'S *BEGGAR'S OPERA*: ITS CONTENT, HISTORY
      AND INFLUENCE (New Haven: 1923)

      A useful scholarly study of all aspects of the opera. Schutz
      discusses the background to the first production; the influence
      of Pope and Swift; the roles of actors and actresses in the
      opera's success; the music, stage history, imitations and suc-
      cessors. Also the opera's political significance.

G5   Irving, William Henry
      JOHN GAY'S LONDON, ILLUSTRATED FROM THE
      POETRY OF THE TIME (Cambridge, Mass.: 1928;
      reprinted 1968)

      Using extensive quotations from Gay and his contemporaries,
      Irving discusses the literary presentation of urban scenes and
      topical issues.

G6 Sherwin, Oscar
MR GAY, BEING A PICTURE OF THE LIFE AND
TIMES OF THE AUTHOR OF *THE BEGGAR'S OPERA*
(New York: 1929)

Attempts something of the style of a showbiz memoire rather
than a literary biography. Impressionistic.

G7 Gaye, Phoebe
JOHN GAY, HIS PLACE IN THE EIGHTEENTH
CENTURY (London: 1938)

A gossipy, unscholarly, unreliable biography which fills in the
factual gaps with colourful surmises.

G8 Irving, William Henry
JOHN GAY, FAVORITE OF THE WITS (Durham,
N. Carolina: 1940)

The best biography of Gay to date. A careful and scholarly
examination of Gay's life and works which makes some sensible
use of the limited documentary materials available. Offers
judicious suggestions to fill in the gaps in our knowledge of
Gay's career, and is particularly good in Gay's relations with his
Scriblerian partners.

G9 Armens, Sven
JOHN GAY, SOCIAL CRITIC (New York: 1954)

Argues forcibly that Gay should be seen not as a miniaturist,
pastoralist or lightweight entertainer, but rather as a serious
and consistent social critic. Analyses the role of money and the
condition of dependency as central themes in Gay's writing.

G10 Forsgren, Adina
JOHN GAY, POET 'OF A LOWER ORDER' (Stockholm:
1964–71), 2 vols.

Reminding us that Johnson's description of Gay as a poet 'of a
lower order' was not intended as disparagement but as an
indication of Gay's success in the minor genres of poetry,

Forsgren demonstrates Gay's inventiveness and skill in pastoral, mock-pastoral and burlesque. Gay, she argues, waged 'a battle for the "little taste" against the "*gusto grande*" '. Sometimes the arguments for Gay's debts to rural sources seem over-scholarly, but this sympathetic study of Gay's skills as an ironic miniaturist and urban balladeer is welcome and perceptive.

G11   Spacks, Patricia Meyer
       JOHN GAY, Twayne *English Authors* series (New York: 1965)

       A useful biographical introduction which studies Gay's development from employing masks as a defence to manipulating them as an attack.

Periodicals and Shorter Articles

G12   Johnson, Samuel
       'Gay', THE LIVES OF THE ENGLISH POETS (London: 1779, 1781) (A71)

       'As a poet', writes Johnson, Gay 'cannot be rated very high. He was, as I once heard a female critic remark, "of a lower order". He had not in any great degree the *mens divinior*, the dignity of genius. Much however must be allowed to the author of a new species of composition, though it be not of the highest kind. We owe to Gay the Ballad Opera; a mode of comedy which at first was supposed to delight only by its novelty, but has now by the experience of half a century been found so well accommodated to the disposition of a popular audience, that it is likely to keep long possession of the stage'.

G13   Thackeray, William Makepeace
       'Prior, Gay and Pope', THE ENGLISH HUMOURISTS OF THE EIGHTEENTH CENTURY (London: 1853)

       Presents Gay as a delightful miniaturist, the creator of 'charming little Dresden china figures'.

G14 Empson, William
'*The Beggar's Opera*, Mock-Pastoral as the Cult of Independence', SOME VERSIONS OF PASTORAL (London: 1935)

A persuasive and influential study which argues that *The Beggar's Opera* celebrates an ironic collaboration between aristocrat and swain in the character of the heroic rogue, at the expense of the bourgeois. 'I should say that the essential process behind the *Opera* was a resolution of heroic and pastoral into a cult of independence'.

G15 Bronson, Bertrand
' "The Beggar's Opera", Studies in the Comic', UNIVERSITY OF CALIFORNIA PUBLICATIONS IN ENGLISH 8, 2 (Berkeley: 1941) 197–231

Examines possible sources, in Handel and in Italian opera, for the musical satire in *The Beggar's Opera*.

G16 Brown, Wallace Cable
'Gay: Pope's Alter Ego', TRIUMPH OF FORM, A STUDY OF THE LATER MASTERS OF THE HEROIC COUPLET (Chapel Hill, N. Carolina: 1948) 45–66

Compares the couplet usage of Pope and Gay and finds, unsurprisingly, many similarities.

G17 Warner, Oliver
'John Gay', WRITERS AND THEIR WORK, 171 (London: 1964)

A disappointing essay. Plentiful quotations from Gay's works, but little critical insight.

G18 Kernan, Alvin B.
THE PLOT OF SATIRE (Yale: 1965) (A21)

Contains an interesting chapter on Gay's *Trivia*.

G19   Battestin, Martin C.
'Menalcas' Song: The Meaning of Art and Artifice in Gay's
Poetry', *JEGP* 65 (1966) 662–79

Excellent study of the interdependence of art and nature in
Gay's form of mock-pastoral comedy.

G20   Kramnick, Isaac
'John Gay – Beggars, Gentry and Society',
BOLINGBROKE AND HIS CIRCLE, THE POLITICS OF
NOSTALGIA IN THE AGE OF WALPOLE (Cambridge,
Mass.: 1968) 223–30

Kramnick sees Gay's mock-pastoral attacks on commercial
values as part of a sustained nostalgic humanist critique of an
emerging capitalist society. Interesting, an essay which does not
condescend to Gay.

G21   Battestin, Martin C.
THE PROVIDENCE OF WIT: ASPECTS OF FORM IN
AUGUSTAN LITERATURE AND THE ARTS (Oxford:
1974) (A41)

Contains a useful chapter on the deceptive metaphorical seriousness of Gay's vocabulary.

G22   Sherbo, Arthur
'John Gay: Lightweight or Heavyweight?', *The Scriblerian*
VIII, 1 (1975) 4–8

Sherbo divides recent critics of Gay into two camps: the 'heavyweights', who see him as a serious social critic; and the
'lightweights', who see him as a charming entertainer. Among
the heavyweights he places Armens (G9), Battestin (G21),
Chalker (A87) and Donaldson (A32). Among the lightweights
he numbers Johnson (G12), Sutherland (A75) and Spacks
(G11).

G23 Nokes, David
'Shepherds and Chimeras'; and 'Businessman, Beggar-Man,
Thief', RAILLERY AND RAGE, A STUDY OF
EIGHTEENTH-CENTURY SATIRE (Brighton: 1987)
(A69) 122–35, 135–49

In 'Shepherds and Chimeras' Nokes looks at *The Shepherd's Week*, with its subtle and playful mingling of tones. In 'Businessman, Beggar-Man, Thief' he analyses the language and imagery of commerce in *The Beggar's Opera*.

Goldsmith, Oliver (1730–74)

Edition

GO1   Friedman, Arthur (ed.)
COLLECTED WORKS OF OLIVER GOLDSMITH
(Oxford: 1966), 5 vols.

The definitive edition of Goldsmith's Collected Works. The introductions and critical notes, though essential to the specialist, are not of general interest, excluding any extensive critical evaluation and concentrating instead on textually related matters such as authorship and variant readings. In his critically conservative introduction to the volume, Friedman dismisses the suggestions by Hopkins (GO11) and others that Goldsmith is a complex artist.

Full-length Studies

GO2   Black, William
GOLDSMITH, *English Men of Letters* series (London: 1878)

A late Victorian study of Goldsmith, more interesting as an example of early criticism than for its interpretation of Goldsmith's life and works.

GO3   Hadow, G. E. and C. B. Wheeler (eds.)
ESSAYS ON GOLDSMITH (Oxford: 1918)

A selection of early critical essays on Goldsmith by Scott, Macaulay and Thackeray. More interesting for its sidelight on late-nineteenth-century criticism than for its approach to Goldsmith himself.

GO4   Gwynn, Stephen L.
OLIVER GOLDSMITH (London: 1935)

A florid and prosey biography of Goldsmith, whom Gwynn describes as 'the ugly duckling of English literature'.

GO5   Freeman, W.
OLIVER GOLDSMITH (London: 1951)

Freeman's biography of Goldsmith serves as an introduction to Goldsmith's friends and associates, for the benefit of readers unfamiliar with the period; his thumbnail sketches are taken directly from the *Dictionary of National Biography*. Freeman's emphasis is on Goldsmith the man; he uses the literary works only as material to support his biographical interpretation.

GO6   Neal, Minnie M.
OLIVER GOLDSMITH (1955)

A brief and chatty biography concerned less with Goldsmith's achievements than with his 'enviable' character.

GO7   Wardle, R. M.
OLIVER GOLDSMITH (Lawrence, Kansas: 1957)

A sympathetic and scholarly approach to Goldsmith's life. Occasionally offers theories based on scant evidence, but makes it scrupulously clear that this is the case.

GO8   Jeffares, A. N.
OLIVER GOLDSMITH, *Writers and Their Works* series (London: 1959)

Includes a brief biography of Goldsmith. The chapter on 'The Poems' is a useful introduction to the subject, though not a critically demanding study.

GO9   Kirk, Clara M.
OLIVER GOLDSMITH, Twayne *English Authors* series (New York: 1967)

A brief study, concentrating on the major works. Considers Goldsmith under five generic headings of essayist, poet, novelist, dramatist and biographer.

GO10 Quintana, R.
OLIVER GOLDSMITH, A GEORGIAN STUDY, *Masters of Literature* series (New York: 1967)

A chronological analysis of Goldsmith's major works, with much useful background information of Goldsmith's life and friendships. Critical analysis covers such topics as Goldsmith's use of a persona in the essays, and the Virgilian conventions of *The Deserted Village*.

GO11 Hopkins, Robert H.
THE TRUE GENIUS OF OLIVER GOLDSMITH (Baltimore: 1969)

Hopkins challenges traditional assumptions about Goldsmith's character and champions him as the 'man of sense', emphasising satire instead of sentimentalism. *The Vicar of Wakefield* is read as a satiric parody of the gullible parson – not, as liberal humanists have argued, as an imperfect idealist showing the follies of man. Hopkins' provocative study has fuelled further debate on the achievements of Goldsmith.

GO12 Lytton-Sells, Arthur
OLIVER GOLDSMITH: HIS LIFE AND WORKS (London: 1974)

The section on Goldsmith's life is less thorough and perceptive than Wardle's biography (GO7), and relies heavily on nineteenth-century sources. A notable omission is any adequate criticism of Goldsmith's Irish origins and his feelings about his home country. The second half of the book is an attempt at a literary survey organised by genre, but lacks any critical insight, being padded with plot summaries and obscure literary models.

GO13 Rousseau, G. S.
GOLDSMITH: THE CRITICAL HERITAGE (London, Boston: 1974)

In the *Critical Heritage* series, reproducing criticism from Goldsmith's contemporaries to the end of the nineteenth century. Rousseau divides the material into two sections: criticism of the major works; and a chronological selection of statements about Goldsmith the man and his works in general.

GO14 Ginger, John
THE NOTABLE MAN: THE LIFE AND TIMES OF OLIVER GOLDSMITH (London: 1977)

Ginger approaches Goldsmith's texts as source material for a psychological biography rather than as literary works in their own right. His interpretation of Goldsmith's character is interesting and perceptive, however, and his book provides a valuable introduction to Goldsmith's life.

GO15 Swarbrick, Andrew (ed.)
THE ART OF OLIVER GOLDSMITH (London: 1984)

A collection of ten essays on poetry, drama and novels. As a poet, he assesses Goldsmith's difficult place in literary history between neo-classical and Johnsonian traditions. Of particular interest are the essays by John Montague on *The Deserted Village* ('The Sentimental Prophecy'); Pat Rogers, 'The Dialectic of *The Traveller*'; and J. A. Downie, 'Goldsmith, Swift and Augustan Satirical Verse'.

Periodicals and Shorter Articles

GO16 Eversole, Richard
'The Oratorical Design of *The Deserted Village*', *ELN* iv (1966) 99–104

Eversole interprets *The Deserted Village* as following 'the structural rules of a classical oration'.

GO17 Rodway, Alan
'Goldsmith and Sheridan: Satirists of Sentiment', RENAISSANCE AND MODERN ESSAYS (ed. G. R. Hibbard) (London: 1966) 65–72

Although mainly concerned with drama, this essay provides a useful reminder that Goldsmith could write satirically. Rodway explores the paradox that while these two writers were purportedly concerned to resurrect Restoration drama, they were 'affected by the usurping Genteel or Sentimental mode' they were also attacking.

GO18   Dussinger, John A.
'Oliver Goldsmith, Citizen of the World', *Studies on Voltaire and the Eighteenth Century* lv (1967) 445–61

Analyses the influence of Locke's empiricism on Goldsmith's philosophy.

GO19   Jack, Ian
'The Deserted Village', *New Rambler* III series c (June 1967) 2–4

An abstract of a Johnson Society paper. A general discussion of the literary, social and historical significance of *The Deserted Village*.

GO20   Friedman, Arthur
'Aspects of Sentimentalism in Eighteenth-Century Literature', THE AUGUSTAN AGE (Oxford: 1970) 247–61

Friedman opens his discussion with Goldsmith's remarks about sentimental comedy: the central figure as a paragon of virtue and the effect that this figure has on the audience. The theme of sentimentalism, rather than detailed literary analysis, is the dominant subject of the essay.

GO21   Quintana, R.
'Oliver Goldsmith, Ironist to the Georgians', EIGHTEENTH-CENTURY STUDIES IN HONOUR OF DONALD F. HYDE (ed. W. F. Bond) (New York: 1970) 297–310

A major essay of Goldsmith scholarship, written for the specialist rather than the student. Quintana interprets Goldsmith as a Georgian (rather than, more generally, as an Augustan), 'representative of his period'. He highlights Goldsmith's linguistic subtleties and stresses their significance for parody and burlesque.

GO22 Storm, Leo F.
'Literary Convention in Goldsmith's *Deserted Village*', *HLQ*
33 (1970) 243–56

Storm argues that *The Deserted Village* is not a personal
reflection but an example of highly conventional poetry, combining the traditions of topographical writing and georgic verse.

GO23 Backman, Sven
THIS SINGULAR TALE: A STUDY OF THE VICAR OF
WAKEFIELD AND ITS LITERARY BACKGROUND,
Lund Studies in English, 40 (Lund, 1971)

Backman's approach to Goldsmith is subtle and intelligent. He
provides an excellent survey of Goldsmith scholarship in the
context of the history of criticism, and his own critical exploration is stimulating and original. Especially useful in his discussion of Goldsmith's relationship to contemporary genres such
as the 'rogue' novel.

GO24 Ferguson, Oliver W.
'Goldsmith's "Retaliation" ', *SAQ* 70 (1971) 149–60

After a promising opening about the complex nature of this
little-known poem, Ferguson's essay achieves little in the way
of literary analysis but does add some minor details to our
biographical knowledge of Goldsmith.

GO25 Jaarsma, Richard J.
'Ethics in the Wasteland: Image and Structure in *The
Deserted Village*', *TSLL* 13 (1971) 446–59

Jaarsma approaches *The Deserted Village* as a poem which
manipulates conventions in order to impose order on the
material.

GO26 Hume, Robert D.
'Goldsmith and Sheridan and the Supposed Revolution of
"Laughing" Against "Sentimental" Comedy', STUDIES IN

CHANGE AND REVOLUTION (ed. Paul J. Korshin) (Menston, Yorkshire: 1972) 237–76

A survey of theatrical fashions 1760–80, looking at changing tastes in comedy and concluding that 'Laughing Comedy' remained the most popular genre. Argues that Goldsmith and Sheridan should not be classed together as supposed objectors to this genre.

GO27 Goldstein, Laurence
'The Auburn Syndrome: Change and Loss in *The Deserted Village* and Wordsworth's Grasmere', *ELH* 40 (1973) 352–71

Wordsworth's poetry seen as an attempt to solve the problems posed by Goldsmith in 'the irreversible dislocation of his past and present'.

GO28 Helgerson, Richard
'The Two Worlds of Oliver Goldsmith', *SEL* 13 (1973) 516–34

Helgerson emphasises Goldsmith the satirist, pointing to the ironic possibilities of his linguistic inversions.

GO29 Hunting, Robert
'The Poems in *The Vicar of Wakefield*', *Criticism* 15 (1973) 234–41

Hunting argues for a revisionist reading of Goldsmith which recognises the possibilities for ironic strategy. He suggests that the two major poems, 'Edwin and Angelina' and 'The Elegy on the Death of a Mad Dog', provide an important instance of Goldsmith's satiric intent when read in the context of the surrounding scenes in the novel.

GO30 Ferguson, Oliver W.
'Doctor Primrose and Goldsmith's Clerical Ideal', *PQ* 54 (Winter 1975) 323–32

An extended consideration of Goldsmith's attitude to the church, and the light that this throws on the character of the Vicar. Ferguson runs into critical difficulties in considering Dr

Primrose as an ironic character separated from his role of narrator.

GO31 Lonsdale, Roger
' "A Garden, and a Grave": The Poetry of Oliver Goldsmith', THE AUTHOR IN HIS WORK: ESSAYS ON A PROBLEM IN CRITICISM (ed. Louis L. Martz and Aubrey Williams) (New Haven, London: 1978)

Lonsdale offers a sensitive approach to *The Traveller* and *The Deserted Village* in this closely argued opening essay of the volume. He interprets the poems as being in some sense 'autobiographical' rather than emphasising Goldsmith's 'rhetorical strategies'.

Gray, Thomas (1716–71)

Bibliographies and Editions

GR1   Starr, Herbert W.
A BIBLIOGRAPHY OF THOMAS GRAY 1917–51
(Philadelphia: 1953)

A bibliography of critical writings on Thomas Gray.

GR2   Starr, H. W. and J. R. Hendrickson (eds.)
THE COMPLETE POEMS OF THOMAS GRAY (Oxford:
1966)

The definitive edition of Gray's works, including English, Latin
and Greek poems. Includes Kittredge's influential essay on the
Norse poems. With this exception, however, the commentary is
largely confined to scholarly queries and is not of general
interest to the student.

GR3   Lonsdale, Roger
THOMAS GRAY AND WILLIAM COLLINS: POETICAL
WORKS (Oxford: 1977)

An extremely useful edition of the poetical works of Gray and
Collins, for the student. Lonsdale's extensive commentary and
notes are informative and reliable.

Full-length Studies

GR4   Golden, Morris
THOMAS GRAY, Twayne *English Authors* series (New
York: 1964)

Combines a brief life of the poet with some background information and a fairly traditional appreciation of the poems. A
useful summary of historical contexts and critical views.

GR5   Starr, Herbert W. (ed.)
ELEGY WRITTEN IN A COUNTRY CHURCHYARD,
Merrill Literary Casebook series (Columbus, Ohio: 1968)

Includes a helpful though selective critical bibliography.
Among the book's useful contents are the 1785 essay by John
Scott of Amwell, and an expanded version of a paper first
published by Starr in *JEGP* in 1946.

GR6   Starr, Herbert W. (ed.)
TWENTIETH-CENTURY INTERPRETATIONS OF
GRAY'S *ELEGY* (Englewood Cliffs: 1968)

A collection of critical essays, with a useful sample of early
criticism of the poem.

GR7   Downey, James and Ben Jones (eds.)
FEARFUL JOY: PAPERS FROM THE THOMAS GRAY
BICENTENARY CONFERENCE AT CARLETON
UNIVERSITY (McGill–Queen's University Press, 1974)

A collection of papers on the life and works of Thomas Gray.
As the editors note in their Preface, the collection presents a
one-sided view of Gray, concentrating on his melancholia
rather than his humour. Hagstrum on 'Gray's Sensibility' emphasises the poet's sensitivity; Tracey stresses the influence of
the elegaic tradition; Johnston analyses Gray's stylistic innova-
tions; Greene comments on the archaisms of Gray's poetic
diction and recounts inaccurate anecdotes about his under-
graduate escapades. Other papers include an introduction to
the correspondence, by Ian Jack; Kenneth Maclean on Gray's
poetic imagery; and Irene Taylor on illustrations to Gray's
poems.

GR8   Lytton-Sells, Arthur
THOMAS GRAY, HIS LIFE AND WORKS (London:
1980)

Lytton-Sells organises his material into two sections. The first
covers biographical information, but in fact achieves little
beyond a generalised and inaccurate account of life in the
eighteenth century; what factual information on Gray he does

supply is, however, generally reliable. The second section is a survey of Gray's various literary activities as a letter-writer, Latin poet, English poet and translator. Overall, Lytton-Sells is not sympathetic to Gray as a man or as a poet: his writing is, he argues, 'limited and indecisive, like his life'. The study contains very little original interpretation, and fundamentally misunderstands Gray's achievements.

Periodicals and Shorter Articles

GR9   Brady, Frank
'Structure and Meaning in Gray's *Elegy*', FROM SENSIBILITY TO ROMANTICISM (ed. F. W. Hilles and H. Bloom) (New York: 1965) 177–89

'After two hundred years not merely are the poem's structure and meaning matters of debate, but no general agreement exists about who is saying what to whom', Brady begins. The *Elegy* is thus 'far from being a simple poem composed of noble commonplaces', but 'an unexpected example of T. S. Eliot's assertion that poetry can communicate before it is understood'.

GR10   Bronson, Bertrand H.
'On a Special Decorum in Gray's *Elegy*', FROM SENSIBILITY TO ROMANTICISM (ed. F. W. Hilles and H. Bloom (New York: 1965) 171–6

Bronson believes that Gray shared with the Augustans a sense of morality gracefully underlying all of creation. Although he was aware of the formal 'rules' of this system, Bronson argues that Gray's interpretation of them was closer to instinct than to deliberate application.

GR11   Jack, Ian
'Gray's *Elegy* Reconsidered', FROM SENSIBILITY TO ROMANTICISM (ed. F. W. Hilles and H. Bloom) (New York: 1965) 139–69

'There are two different sorts of poem', Ian Jack rather surprisingly begins: 'poems whose writers know from the beginning what they intend to say: and poems whose writers do not'. On the basis of these categories, Jack proceeds to argue that Gray did not deliberately plan the *Elegy*, but was overpowered by the forces of his imagination and produced a poem 'born of a mood'.

GR12 Spacks, Patricia Meyer
'Statement and Artifice in Thomas Gray', *SEL* v (1965) 519–32

Discusses the role of 'artificial' or elaborate diction in Gray's poetry and the changing tastes of readers in connection with poetic theories, which render such poetry 'unacceptable' to critics as diverse as Wordsworth, Coleridge and F. R. Leavis.

GR13 Vernon, P. F.
'The Structure of Gray's Early Poems', *Essays in Criticism* xv (1965) 381–93

Argues that Gray's use of symbolism in *The Progress of Poesy* and *The Bard*, which struck his contemporaries with 'mute amazement', can be traced through his earlier poems whose complexity has been overlooked in the emphasis on the 'reflective' nature of the verses.

GR14 Johnston, Arthur
THOMAS GRAY AND 'THE BARD' (Cardiff: 1966)

A brief study of Gray's use of the primitive.

GR15 Spacks, Patricia Meyer
' "Artful Strife": Conflict in Gray's Poetry', *PMLA* lxxxi (1966) 63–9

Discusses the concluding lines of *The Progress of Poesy*, with their use of the antithesis of Good and Great, as the metaphor for understanding 'a conflict vital to his most compelling effects'. Surveys contemporary reactions to the weaknesses of Gray's poetry, and the relationship between his 'reflective' stances and his essentially moral preoccupations.

GR16   Ellis, Frank H.
'Gray's *Eton College Ode*: The Problem of Tone', *Papers on Language and Literature* v (1969) 130–8

Ellis argues that Gray's *Ode* mixes the tones of farce and melancholy found elsewhere in his work; this mixed tone, he suggests, 'enables the poem to confront the real desolations of manhood'.

GR17   Lonsdale, Roger
'The Poetry of Thomas Gray: Versions of the Self', Chatterton Lecture on an English Poet 1973 (London: 1973)

Examines the different 'selves' in Gray's poetry; the poet as observer of the human condition, and the poet as alienated outsider to the pastoral scene. Argues that the rewriting of the *Elegy* united these, creating a poetic voice which allowed subsequent verse its greater unity and maturity.

GR18   Jones, Myrddin
'Gray, Jaques, and the Man of Feeling', *RES* n.s. 25 (1974) 39–48

Compares the closing stanzas of Gray's *Elegy* with Jaques' speech in *As You Like It*, on the Seven Ages of Man.

GR19   Sugg, Richard
'The Importance of Voice: Gray's *Elegy*', *Tennessee Studies in Literature* 19 (1974) 115–20

Sees the poem as a structural unity, juxtaposing 'sound and silence': 'Many of the personifications depend upon the fact that the living speak and the dead do not'. Discusses the use of these personifications as part of Gray's mythological allusions.

GR20   Watson, George
'The Voice of Gray', *Critical Quarterly* vol. 19, no. 4 (1977) 51–7

'Gray was a passionate pedant with language', Watson argues, looking at the unusual, 'temperamental' use of language in

Gray's poetry and analysing the complexities of its 'active' and 'passive' voices.

GR21 Wright, George T.
'Stillness and the Argument of Gray's *Elegy*', *MP* 74 (1977) 381–9

Wright suggests that the apparently simple moral of the *Elegy Written in a Country Churchyard*, that the poet is renouncing ambition and aligning himself with the humble poor, is in fact more complex. The style and language of the epitaph, he argues, continue to mark the poet as a sophisticate.

GR22 Micklus, Robert
'Voices in the Wind: The Eton Ode's Ambivalent Prospect of Maturity', *ELN* 18 (1981) 181–6

A close reading of Gray's *Eton College Ode*, which suggests that there is 'nothing inherently ironic' in the description of Eton life: 'The voice of fancy seeks repeatedly to portray Eton not as a world of fleeting allusions, but as a bedrock of stability'.

Johnson, Samuel (1709–84)

As indicated in 'Advice to the Reader', this is a highly selective section, including only those works which deal wholly, or largely, with Johnson's career as a poet.

Editions

J1 McAdam, E. L., jun. and George Milne (eds.) SAMUEL JOHNSON'S POEMS, *The Yale Edition of the Works of Samuel Johnson*, vol. VI (New Haven, London: 1964)

A comprehensive edition of Johnson's poetry. Useful for specialists who require bibliographical information, but more technical in its critical apparatus than most students will need.

J2 Rudd, Niall (ed.)
JOHNSON'S JUVENAL: 'LONDON' AND 'THE VANITY OF HUMAN WISHES' (Bristol: 1981)

An edition of the texts together with explanatory notes.

Full-length Studies

J3 Hilles, Frederick W.
NEW LIGHT ON DR JOHNSON: ESSAYS ON THE OCCASION OF HIS 250TH BIRTHDAY (New Haven: 1959; London: 1960)

The essays in this volume have two major areas of concern: Johnson's life and his poetry. John Butt on 'Johnson's Practice in Poetic Imitation' emphasises 'the grandeur of generality' as a characteristic of Johnson's Juvenal poems. Mary Lascelles covers some of the same ground, though providing a more detailed reading of the classical poet and analysing the differences between Johnson and Juvenal; she sees *The Vanity of*

Human Wishes as 'a great tragic poem'. Nichol Smith suggests that Johnson's verse writing has a spontaneous quality, revealing aspects of his character concealed in the more 'public' genres. Bronson discusses eighteenth-century poetic conventions, and Abrams looks at Johnson's views on poetic metre.

J4 Sachs, Ariel
    PASSIONATE INTELLIGENCE: IMAGINATION AND
    REASON IN THE WORKS OF SAMUEL JOHNSON
    (Baltimore: 1967)

Stressing the influence of Christian pessimism on Johnson's moral outlook, Sachs traces a pattern of polarised antitheses in his works between the impulses of the imagination and the control of reason. Argues that such polarities produce a thematic unity in such works as *The Vanity of Human Wishes* and *Rasselas*.

J5 Cunningham, J. S.
    JOHNSON: *THE VANITY OF HUMAN WISHES* AND
    RASSELAS (London: 1982)

In this brief study of the two works Cunningham offers an excellent introduction to the critical issues they raise, guiding the student reader through a close textual analysis. Parallels are drawn with the periodical essays of *The Rambler*, suggesting Johnson's recurrent moral themes, and reflecting on the cumulative effects of the narrative through such headings as 'Fate', 'Laughter' and 'Stories'. While not presupposing extensive knowledge of Johnson's works, Cunningham encourages the beginner to explore further – though the concluding list of 'Further Reading' is of limited use to the student of poetry, concentrating largely on *Rasselas*.

J6 Grundy, Isobel (ed.)
    SAMUEL JOHNSON: NEW CRITICAL ESSAYS
    (London, New York: 1985)

An interesting volume including valuable essays by Grundy herself on Johnson's use of maxims; by Robert Gildings on Johnson's politics; and by Howard Erskine-Hill on Boswell's *Life of Johnson*.

J7   Grundy, Isobel
      SAMUEL JOHNSON AND THE SCALE OF
      GREATNESS (Leicester: 1986)

      A careful and scholarly study of the significance of the use of the
      terms 'greatness' and 'littleness', together with their synonyms,
      throughout Johnson's writings. A specialist work, but with
      some useful insights for the general reader.

Periodicals

J8   Jack, Ian
      'The "Choice of Life" in Johnson and Matthew Prior', *JEGP*
      xlix (1950) 523–30

      Jack suggests that Johnson was impressed and influenced by
      Solomon.

J9   White, Ian
      'The Vanity of Human Wishes', *CAM Q* 6 (1973) 115–25

      Challenges the traditional pairing of *Rasselas* and *The Vanity of
      Human Wishes* as works sharing a common moral theme, and
      seeks to emphasise the latter as a major work in its own right.

J10   Amis, George T.
      'The Style of *The Vanity of Human Wishes*', *MLQ* 35 (1974)
      16–29

      A brief but perceptive essay which discusses, though not in any
      detail, aspects of vocabulary and verse structure.

Pope, Alexander (1688–1744)

Bibliographies and Editions

P1   Butt, John (gen. ed.)
THE TWICKENHAM EDITION OF THE POEMS OF
ALEXANDER POPE (1939 to 1969), 11 vols.

This exemplary scholarly edition of Pope's poems brings together the editorial and critical skills of the leading Pope
scholars of a generation. Several of the introductory essays,
such as Mack's introduction to the *Essay on Man* (vol. III i) and
to the *Translations of Homer* (vols. VII–X), have the critical
authority and depth of books in their own right. Geoffrey
Tillotson edits *The Rape of the Lock* (vol. II); James Sutherland
edits *The Dunciad* (vol. V); and John Butt edits the *Imitations
of Horace* (vol. IV).

P2   Guerinot, J. V.
PAMPHLET ATTACKS ON ALEXANDER POPE, 1711–
1744: A DESCRIPTIVE BIBLIOGRAPHY (London, New
York: 1969)

Contains 158 items attacking Pope, beginning with John Dennis
and ending with Colley Cibber. Each item is fully annotated,
with lengthy quotations from the most memorable and vi-
tuperative passages. A valuable work in helping modern
readers to comprehend Pope's adversarial attitude towards the
'dunces' throughout his major satires.

P3   Lopez, Cecilia L.
ALEXANDER POPE: AN ANNOTATED
BIBLIOGRAPHY, 1945–67 (Gainesville, Florida: 1970)

P4   Kowalk, Wolfgang
ALEXANDER POPE, AN ANNOTATED
BIBLIOGRAPHY OF TWENTIETH-CENTURY
CRITICISM (Frankfurt: 1981)

Full-length Studies

P5   Warton, Joseph
      AN ESSAY ON THE GENIUS AND WRITINGS OF
      POPE (London: 1756), 2 vols.

Although frequently praising Pope, arguing that several passages in *The Rape of the Lock* 'excel anything in Shakespeare,
or in any other author', this celebrated essay sets the tone for
the later downgrading of Pope by Romantic and nineteenth-
century critics. 'For Wit and Satire are transitory and perish-
able, but Nature and Passion are eternal', writes Warton,
finding too much art in Pope and insufficient nature.

P6   Warren, Austin
      ALEXANDER POPE AS CRITIC AND HUMANIST
      (Princeton: 1929)

A study of Pope as critic, editor, translator, humanist and
scholar. The aim is to demonstrate that Pope's views on culture,
philosophy and art are 'richer and more liberal' than nineteenth-century critics would acknowledge. An important book
in the steady rehabilitation of Pope's reputation from the 1920s
to the present.

P7   Sherburn, George
      THE EARLY CAREER OF ALEXANDER POPE
      (Oxford: 1934)

Until the appearance of Mack's full-length biography in 1985
(P58), Sherburn's account of Pope's early career (up to 1727)
was the best biographical study of the poet available. In some
ways it still offers a more judicious, balanced and analytical
view of Pope's early years than Mack's colourful interpretation.
A sound scholar, Sherburn weaves a mass of factual details into
an engaging and stimulating narrative. A book without flour-
ishes, but full of insight and understanding, which offers an
excellent analysis of Pope's relationships with friends and foes
in this period of his life.

P8   Root, Robert Kilburn
      THE POETICAL CAREER OF ALEXANDER POPE
      (Princeton: 1938)

      Somewhat leisurely and old-fashioned in approach, this book
      still has occasional insights. Follows a chronological pattern to
      illustrate 'the progress of a literary career'. Interesting, but
      represents a kind of approach that was superseded by the more
      rigorous critical style of the New Critics.

P9   Tillotson, Geoffrey
      ON THE POETRY OF POPE (Oxford: 1938)

      Although now seeming rather old-fashioned, Tillotson's influ-
      ential study is a sensitive and detailed examination of some
      central features of Pope's poetry. His book is dominated by the
      notion of 'correctness'. Each of the chapters – on Nature,
      Design, Language and Versification – is presented as a varia-
      tion on this central theme of correctness. This now appears a
      rather narrow and formal preoccupation, but Tillotson presents
      his argument with insight and skill.

P10   Ault, Norman
      NEW LIGHT ON POPE (London: 1949)

      One of the most significant contributions to post-war scholar-
      ship on Pope. In a series of separate studies, Ault sheds new
      light on some of the most vexed issues in Pope's life and career,
      incidentally introducing some previously unknown additions to
      the canon of his poetry. He examines Pope's relationships with
      Addison, Rowe, Cibber and Swift, in each case separating fact
      from legend. A model of careful research and sound
      judgement.

P11   Knight, Douglas
      POPE AND THE HEROIC TRADITION (New Haven:
      1951)

      Taking his cue from Pope's observation that 'if I had not
      undertaken that work [the translation of Homer], I should
      certainly have writ an epic', Knight examines the translation as
      a piece of original poetry. He studies both the local verbal

achievement of Pope's work, and the general cumulative effects. Examining the poem's embodiment of a heroic tradition, Knight pays particular attention to the blending of Homeric and Christian ideas. It is a fascinating short book for the serious student of this area of Pope's work. Its influence can be seen in Maynard Mack's introduction to the *Iliad* volume in the Twickenham Edition of the works of Pope.

P12   Knight, G. Wilson
LAUREATE OF PEACE, OR THE GENIUS OF
ALEXANDER POPE (London: 1954)

Idiosyncratic, as all Wilson Knight's criticism tends to be; sometimes inspired, at other times awkward. His chapter on 'The Vital Flame' examines Pope's poetic evocation of nature by comparison and analogy with many other English poets. For much of the book Wilson Knight discusses Pope and Byron side by side.

P13   Parkin, Rebecca Price
THE POETIC WORKMANSHIP OF ALEXANDER
POPE (Minneapolis: 1955)

In her preface Parkin writes: 'In Pope's poetic universe all sins, both mortal and venial, stem from solipsism'. However, her route to an understanding of Pope's morality is via a detailed analysis of his poetic technique. She examines his use of such devices as the implied dramatic speaker, irony, tension, parallelism, antithesis, paradox, narrative, metaphor and tonal variations. Careful and enthusiastic, Parkin's book is one of a number of such sympathetic studies in the 1940s and 1950s which helped to pave the way for the high critical reputation which Pope now enjoys.

P14   Rogers, Robert W.
THE MAJOR SATIRES OF ALEXANDER POPE
(Urbana, Illinois: 1955)

Another work setting out to challenge and reverse nineteenth-century prejudices about Pope, 'one of the most controversial English poets'. Rogers still feels it necessary to insist that 'basically [Pope] was sincere and honest'. A sincere and honest book, but its critical analyses have been largely superseded by the more detailed work of later critics.

P15 Williams, Aubrey
POPE'S *DUNCIAD*, A STUDY OF ITS MEANING
(London: 1955)

An important study, which illustrates the depth of allusion in Pope's great mock-heroic satire. Williams shows how verbal echoes from the *Aeneid* blend with processional details from the Lord Mayor's Show to create the multi-layered satiric texture of the poem. Informative, eloquent and perceptive.

P16 Tillotson, Geoffrey
POPE AND HUMAN NATURE (Oxford: 1958)

Following the formal preoccupations of Tillotson's earlier work on the poetry of Pope (1938; P9), this book is 'mainly about the material Pope expresses'. Tillotson discusses Pope's views on Man, Nature, Truth, The Beautiful and The Ugly. He illustrates his arguments with plentiful quotations. Judicious and informative.

P17 Brower, Reuben Arthur
ALEXANDER POPE: THE POETRY OF ALLUSION
(Oxford: 1959)

This is the most thorough and scholarly analysis of Pope's use of classical borrowings and imitations. Brower argues that Pope was 'perhaps the last major English poet to feel at home with the whole European and English tradition in poetry' (p. 353). He examines the influence of Theocritus and Virgil on Pope's *Pastorals*, *The Rape of the Lock* and *Windsor Forest*; and of Ovid on *The Elegy to an Unfortunate Lady*, *Eloisa to Abelard* and *The Rape of the Lock*. He finds echoes of the *Aeneid* throughout Pope's poetry, and the general influence of Horace is also all-pervasive. However, Brower does not confine his attention to spotting parallels and discovering sources. His aim is to show 'how he used the poetry of the past for his own expressive purposes'. The book contains many excellent passages of close literary analysis which demonstrate the imaginative coalition of past and present, source and imitation.

P18   Wasserman, Earl R.
POPE'S EPISTLE TO BATHURST: A CRITICAL
READING WITH AN EDITION OF THE
MANUSCRIPTS (Baltimore: 1960)

An ingenious study in which Wasserman deciphers the inter-
woven traditions of Horatian *sermo* and Christian sermon in
Pope's satire. The poem, he argues, is what Horace 'would have
written had he known the divine word'. Wasserman combines
subtle verbal analysis with a wealth of contextual evidence to
establish the 'climate of attitudes' surrounding Pope's philosophical outlook.

P19   Boyce, Benjamin
THE CHARACTER SKETCHES IN POPE'S POEMS
(Durham, N. Carolina: 1962)

Boyce argues that 'attention to the "total" design, to poetic
texture and to the personae of the major poems has somehow
mostly left out of consideration the schemes and traditions of
his character-sketches'. His study concentrates on Pope's
choice of subjects, the revisions of his character-sketches, his
poetic models, his technique and the significance of a doctrine
such as 'the ruling passion' in his delineation of character. He
concludes: 'In the sketching of these figures he departed from
neo-classicism to inhabit the larger world of free and illimitable
surprise'.

P20   Edwards, Thomas R., jun.
THIS DARK ESTATE: A READING OF POPE,
Perspectives in Literature series, 11 (Berkeley, Los Angeles:
1963)

Tracing a line of development from Pope's earliest poems to the
final version of *The Dunciad* in 1743, Edwards argues that
Pope's poetic career demonstrates a movement away from the
concordia discors of the 'Augustan mode', to a more 'gro-
tesque' style of personal bitterness and anger. Where the earlier
poems offer a classical synthesis of moral idealism and satiric
realism, the late poems, he argues – though 'less pure and
structurally less "perfect" ' – have greater force and power.

P21 Adler, Jacob H.
THE REACH OF ART: A STUDY OF THE PROSODY
OF POPE (Gainesville, Florida: 1964)

An analysis of Pope's prosodic techniques as they varied from
poem to poem throughout his career. Adler concludes: 'The
variety of his verses is astonishingly wide; subtle variations in
tone color, in caesural quality and quantity, in the weight of a
line and the beats within it; unusual lightness and swiftness,
unusual heaviness and sonority; fine gradual effortless crescen-
does and diminuendoes.'

P22 Mack, Maynard (ed.)
ESSENTIAL ARTICLES FOR THE STUDY OF POPE
(London: 1964; revised 1968)

Although hardly justifying the adjective 'essential', this is
indeed an excellent collection of some of the most celebrated
and influential essays on Pope published between 1946 and
1963. It is impossible to discuss each of the important essays
collected here; instead, there follows a list of some of the main
contributors, each of whom is represented by an essay of major
critical significance: F. R. Leavis, W. H. Auden, S. H. Monk,
W. K. Wimsatt, Austin Warren, Reuben Brower, E. R.
Wasserman, E. N. Hooker, William Empson, J. R. Moore,
Cleanth Brooks, Aubrey Williams, Ian Jack, Norman Ault,
John Butt, J. M. Osborn, G. K. Hunter, J. M. Aden, Norman
Callan, Douglas Knight, James Sutherland, R. H. Griffith,
George Sherburn, T. R. Edwards, Alvin Kernan, H. H.
Erskine-Hill.

P23 Maresca, Thomas E.
POPE'S HORATIAN POEMS (Columbus, Ohio: 1966)

Maresca says of his book that 'it is quite simply an investigation
of what the Imitations of Horace are about'. Beginning with a
study of Horace's significance for Augustan readers, he offers
some tentative ethical and aesthetic theories which point to a
Christianised transformation of the Latin poet. Throughout the
book he prefers rhetorical questions to answers, and although
always intelligent and interesting, his work offers few original
insights.

P24   Spence, Joseph
OBSERVATIONS, ANECDOTES AND CHARACTERS
OF BOOKS AND MEN (ed. J. M. Osborn) (Oxford: 1966),
2 vols.

Originally begun in the 1740s, Spence's *Anecdotes* provide
much of the raw material for many subsequent biographies of
Pope, as well as detailed and idiosyncratic insights into other
authors of the period. Mainly culled from conversation with
Pope, the anecdotes discuss his relations with such contemporaries as Addison, Swift, Lady Mary Wortley Montagu and
Hervey, as well as subjects ranging from landscape gardening to
painting. Osborn's edition, which presents 1,648 separate anecdotes, is a masterpiece of scholarship.

P25   Kallich, Martin I.
HEAV'NS FIRST LAW: RHETORIC AND ORDER IN
POPE'S *ESSAY ON MAN* (DeKalb, Illinois: 1967)

This book combines a summary of received opinions on the
Essay on Man with some new thoughts on certain key concepts
such as Providence and Bliss. The 'first law' of the title is Order,
and Kallich explores some verbal ambiguities in Pope's presentation of the perfect order of creation. There is a tendency to
explain any poetic and doctrinal contradictions by invoking the
antithetical formulas of neo-classicism.

P26   Dixon, Peter
THE WORLD OF POPE'S SATIRES (London: 1968)

A perceptive and eloquent study of Pope and the context of his
satires. Dixon discusses such issues as the topicality and al-
lusiveness of Pope's satires, the Horatian model of gentlemanly
conduct, and country virtues. His comments on court life and
'the trading interest' as presented in the poems are judicious, if
brief. Concludes with chapters on 'The Stoic's Pride' and
'Discords and Harmonies'. A useful book for students.

P27   Hunt, John Dixon
       THE RAPE OF THE LOCK, A CASEBOOK (London:
       1968)

       A useful compendium of some of the most celebrated and
       influential essays on *The Rape of the Lock*, from John Dennis's
       notorious attack (1728) to Martin Price's subtle exploration of
       'The Problem of Scale: The Game of Art' (1946). Also included
       are essays by G. Wilson Knight, Geoffrey Tillotson, Cleanth
       Brooks, Maynard Mack, Reuben Brower, Aubrey Williams
       and J. S. Cunningham. An excellent conspectus of critical views
       on this much-studied poem.

P28   Nicolson, Marjorie and G. S. Rousseau
       'THIS LONG DISEASE, MY LIFE'; ALEXANDER POPE
       AND THE SCIENCES (Princeton: 1968)

       A fascinating and well-researched study of Pope's attitudes to a
       number of medical and scientific subjects, ranging from astron-
       omy to blood transfusions. Informative and lively.

P29   Aden, John M.
       SOMETHING LIKE HORACE: STUDIES IN THE ART
       AND ALLUSION OF POPE'S HORATIAN SATIRES
       (Nashville: 1969)

       This book attempts to extend the 'frontier' of our understand-
       ing of Pope's Horatian poems. Paying particular attention to
       the different voices presented in these poems, Aden dis-
       tinguishes between the satirist's own persona, the figure of the
       interlocutor or satiric adversary, and that of the 'prolocutor'
       whose sentiments broaden the satirist's views into a kind of
       civilised consensus. It is a work of close reading and detailed
       analysis, aimed at demonstrating that Pope is 'the only great
       satirist' to show 'a sense of the dignity of satire'.

P30   Jones, John A.
       POPE'S COUPLET ART (Athens, Ohio: 1969)

       In attempting to demonstrate the flexibility of Pope's use of the
       heroic couplet, Jones sets himself the following objectives:

1. To show how and why Pope adopts different couplet norms for different poems.
2. To explain Pope's development as a stylist.
3. To offer some tentative conclusions about the nature and significance of Pope's art as a couplet poet.

As he moves from the earlier to the later poems, Jones finds an 'opening up' or 'mellowing' of Pope's couplet style as 'the spring of Pope's wit has a longer recoil'. An excellent study of both the development and variety of Pope's uses of the couplet.

P31   Mack, Maynard
THE GARDEN AND THE CITY: RETIREMENT AND POLITICS IN THE LATER POETRY OF POPE, 1731–43
(London: 1969)

An imaginative and subtle work of literary interpretation which takes Pope's life of Horatian retirement at Twickenham as the key to an understanding of his political attitudes in the later satires. Demonstrating, with the aid of lavish illustrations, Pope's love of landscape gardening and architecture, Mack argues that Twickenham with its garden and grotto represents a 'rallying point' for Pope's image of himself as philosopher and poet. In opposition to this the City, representing the administration of Walpole and George II, becomes a focus of corruption and anarchy. Mack presents Pope and Walpole, each surrounded by his own symbolic iconography, as two 'mighty opposites' embodying the polarities of light and dark, order and mock-order.

P32   White, Douglas H.
POPE AND THE CONTEXT OF CONTROVERSY: THE MANIPULATION OF IDEAS IN 'AN ESSAY ON MAN'
(Chicago: 1970)

Sets out to 'describe the intellectual climate relevant to some of Pope's important ideas' in the *Essay on Man*. Defends Pope against charges of intellectual shallowness.

P33   Bateson, F. W. and N. A. Joukovsky
ALEXANDER POPE, A CRITICAL ANTHOLOGY
(London: 1971)

Like the *Critical Heritage* volume (P39), this work begins with an anthology of contemporary criticism of Pope by such figures as John Dennis and Lady Mary Wortley Montagu. Unlike *Critical Heritage*, though, it also includes a generous selection of nineteenth-century views, presenting observations by Coleridge, Macaulay and Arnold. It concludes with an enterprising selection of extracts from modern essays by such figures as William Empson, Marshall McLuhan and Donald Davie. An excellent book giving a sound impression of Pope's fluctuating critical reputation.

P34   Spacks, Patricia Meyer
AN ARGUMENT OF IMAGES: THE POETRY OF
ALEXANDER POPE (Cambridge, Mass., London: 1971)

A detailed and sensitive study of Pope's use of metaphor. Sometimes a little narrow in its deliberate neglect of context, but contains a valuable study of figurative vocabulary in the *Essay on Man*.

P35   Dixon, Peter (ed.)
ALEXANDER POPE, *Writers and Their Background*
(London: 1972)

An excellent contextual volume, containing nine valuable essays, each by a different critic on an individual aspect of Pope's life, works and society. The essays are: 'On Reading Pope' by G. S. Rousseau; 'Pope, God and Man' by A. R. Humphreys; 'Pope and the Social Scene' by Pat Rogers; 'Pope and the Visual Arts' by James Sambrook; 'Pope and Politics' by John M. Aden; 'Pope and the Financial Revolution' by Howard Erskine-Hill; 'Pope and the Classics' by Norman Callan; 'Pope and Criticism' by Duncan Isles; and 'Pope and the Idea of Fame' by Donald Fraser.

P36   Erskine-Hill, Howard
POPE, *THE DUNCIAD*, *Studies in English Literature*
(London: 1972)

A brisk and highly informative guidebook to the allusive alleyways and ironic depths of this much misunderstood poem.

P37   Russo, John Paul
ALEXANDER POPE, TRADITION AND IDENTITY
(Cambridge, Mass.: 1972; London: 1973)

By identity Russo means 'the image (Pope) had of himself, and
the figure of himself he set forth in his poetry'. In his treatment
of the interrelationship between Pope's self-image and his
awareness of cultural traditions, Russo stresses Pope's strong
mythopoeic tendency, creating out of his friends and colleagues
a private mythology of Augustan values.

P38   Sitter, John E.
THE POETRY OF POPE'S *DUNCIAD* (Minneapolis,
London: 1972)

Consists of three essays on separate aspects of *The Dunciad*.
The first is critical and examines the 'generic confusion' which
the Goddess of Dulness inspires among her disciples; the
second investigates the possible influence of Sir Richard Black-
more's *Literary Theories* on the poem; and the third traces
parallels between *The Temple of Fame* and *The Dunciad* which
lead Sitter to call the latter poem a 'Temple of Infamy'.

P39   Barnard, John (ed.)
POPE, THE CRITICAL HERITAGE (London, Boston:
1973)

Follows the general pattern of the series, including extracts
from contemporary reviews and letters, starting with Wy-
cherley in 1705 and concluding with Johnson in 1782. Further
contemporary reactions to Pope can be found in Guerinot (P1),
and in F. W. Bateson and N. A. Joukovsky (P33).

P40   Keener, Frederick M.
AN ESSAY ON POPE (New York, London: 1974)

Keener takes as his keynote Pope's observation that 'we care
not to study or to anatomize a poem, but only to read it for our
entertainment'. His essay is elegant, eloquent and subjective.
Deliberately eschewing the erudite display of some commenta-

tors on Pope, he offers a series of brisk, informal and perceptive thoughts on Pope's life and works. Refreshing in its enthusiasm, though there are some weaknesses in this pose of studied amateurism.

P41   Erskine-Hill, Howard
THE SOCIAL MILIEU OF ALEXANDER POPE: LIVES, EXAMPLE AND THE POETIC RESPONSE (New Haven, London: 1975)

In this useful background study, Erskine-Hill examines in meticulous detail the lives of six men who feature as characters in Pope's poetry. Carefully analysing the relationships between fact and fiction, Erskine-Hill illuminates Pope's satiric method. His comments on Pope's ideas concerning the 'use of riches' and on Pope's Jacobite tendencies are particularly interesting. Scholarly and authoritative, a book for the serious student rather than the casual reader.

P42   Rogers, Pat
AN INTRODUCTION TO POPE (London: 1975)

By his use of the word 'introduction', Rogers explains, he has in mind 'the art of sociable courtesy by which we introduce one friend to another'. This brief, brisk and perceptive study has the familiar hallmarks of Rogers' approach. It is lively, witty, full of insight, and displays its wealth of scholarship with disarming modesty. The chapter on 'The Politics of Style' offers a sturdy, unpedantic analysis of Pope's use of the heroic couplet. The chapter on the 'Maze of Humanity' helps the modern reader to find his way through the philosophy of the *Essay on Man* and the four *Moral Essays*. Rogers is particularly skilful at exploring the allusive subtleties in Pope's deceptively simple vocabulary. Probably the best short critical study of Pope for student use.

P43   Gooneratne, Yasmine
ALEXANDER POPE (Cambridge: 1976)

Offers a simplistic critical approach to Pope's major poems for the benefit of less gifted students.

P44   Gordon, I. R. F.
A PREFACE TO POPE (London: 1976)

An intelligent and balanced introductory work for use by
students. Overshadowed by Pat Rogers' simultaneous and
similar *Introduction to Pope* (1975; P42) but still useful.

P45   Leranbaum, Miriam
ALEXANDER POPE'S 'OPUS MAGNUM', 1729–44
(Oxford: 1977)

Leranbaum brings together the many scattered references to a
proposed great moral and ethical poem which haunted Pope's
thinking throughout the last fifteen years of his life. She examines the Lucretian influence on the *Essay on Man* and the
relationship between that *Essay* and the *Moral Essays*. The
book closes with a consideration of Pope's unwritten epic
Brutus.

P46   Aden, John M.
POPE'S ONCE AND FUTURE KINGS: SATIRE AND
POLITICS IN THE EARLY CAREER (Knoxville: 1978)

This study examines the interrelationships of politics, satire and
religion in Pope's early poems. Aden suggests that Pope was
'probably Jacobitical in sentiment, if only wistfully so'. Detailed points, but limited general appeal.

P47   Brownell, Morris R.
ALEXANDER POPE AND THE ARTS OF GEORGIAN
ENGLAND (Oxford: 1978)

Brownell presents Pope under four aspects:

1. As a virtuoso in the Renaissance tradition.
2. As an artist immediately involved in the life of his times.
3. As an aesthetic philosopher who assumed the unity of the
   arts.
4. As a socially responsible citizen who assumed a public
   responsibility for the culture of his time.

A learned volume with a long and interesting chapter on
landscape gardening.

P48   Erskine-Hill, Howard and Anne Smith (eds.)
THE ART OF ALEXANDER POPE (London: 1979)

An interesting, though not outstanding, collection of essays. Best contributions are by Erskine-Hill on Pope's ideas of architecture, and by David Morris on 'civilised reading'. The nine other contributors include Pat Rogers, Felicity Rosslyn and Clive Probyn.

P49   Halsband, Robert
THE RAPE OF THE LOCK AND ITS ILLUSTRATIONS
1714–1896 (Oxford: 1980)

A short book, copiously illustrated, which surveys illustrations of *The Rape of the Lock* from the first appearance of the five-canto version in 1714, until the edition of 1896 'embroidered with nine drawings' by Aubrey Beardsley. Halsband argues that Pope may have had a hand in the 1714 illustrations.

P50   Mack, Maynard and James A. Winn (eds.)
POPE: RECENT ESSAYS BY SEVERAL HANDS
(Brighton: 1980)

Follows on from the volume *Essential Articles for the Study of Pope* (1964, revised 1968; P22). This volume gathers together some of the most important essays of the 1970s on Pope. Its list of contributors makes impressive reading, including: John Butt, Ronald Paulson, Hugh Kenner, Martin Battestin, David Morris, Pat Rogers, Patricia Meyer Spacks, Louis Landa, W. K. Wimsatt, Earl Wasserman, Ian Jack, Howard Erskine-Hill, John Aden, Thomas R. Edwards and Emrys Jones. The level of scholarship and criticism is high, attesting to the enviable status that Pope now enjoys among literary critics.

P51   Mack, Maynard
COLLECTED IN HIMSELF, ESSAYS CRITICAL,
BIOGRAPHICAL AND BIBLIOGRAPHICAL ON POPE
AND SOME OF HIS CONTEMPORARIES (Newark,
London, Toronto: 1982)

This collection of scholarly notes and queries, mainly devoted to aspects of Pope's life and work, brings together many of the findings of Mack's lifetime study of Pope. Collected into this single scholarly volume, the accumulation of bibliographical notes and epistolary revisions represents the kind of detailed academic research which Mack, perhaps unwisely, chose to exclude from his subsequent biography of Pope (P58).

P52   Weinbrot, Howard D.
ALEXANDER POPE AND THE TRADITIONS OF
FORMAL VERSE SATIRE (Princeton: 1982)

Weinbrot examines Pope's transformations of the satiric forms of Horace, Juvenal and Persius to create his own satiric vehicle. He describes Pope's relations with the classical satirists as 'an amiable combat' through which he embraces the classical past in order to differ from it. Pope may imitate Horace, Weinbrot argues, but does not identify well with his values.

P53   Fairer, David
POPE'S IMAGINATION (Manchester: 1984)

Fairer emphasises the subversive and potentially chaotic powers of Pope's imagination. He argues that we should abandon nice distinctions between such terms as 'fancy', 'fantasy', 'imagination' and 'invention' if we are to come to terms with the force of Pope's poetry. He also traces many interesting parallels between Pope's poetic techniques and those of earlier English poets.

P54   Morris, David B.
ALEXANDER POPE, THE GENIUS OF SENSE
(Cambridge, Mass., London: 1984)

An important work which emphasises the role and nature of the poetic judgements presented in Pope's poetry. Morris distinguishes the layers and nuances of meaning contained within the deceptively familiar abstract terms that abound in Pope's verse. His analysis of the importance of Pope's revisions of his poetry is particularly illuminating.

P55   Nuttall, A. D.
POPE'S *ESSAY ON MAN* (London: 1984)

Nuttall describes this study of Pope's philosophy in the *Essay on Man* as 'Crousazian', a polite way of saying hostile. Written in an informal style, this book offers a useful couplet-by-couplet commentary on the poem, reviewing such issues as Pope's concept of equality, the influence on the poem of Pascal, and the strain of determinism running through it. Though at times describing the poem as 'the very nadir of Augustan poetry', Nuttall also makes a number of interesting points on its philosophical axioms.

P56 Brooks-Davies, Douglas
POPE'S *DUNCIAD* AND THE QUEEN OF THE NIGHT: A STUDY IN EMOTIONAL JACOBITISM (Manchester: 1985)

An intriguing but eccentric study which finds coded Jacobite messages throughout Pope's poetry, but particularly in *The Dunciad*. Brooks-Davies presents *The Dunciad* as 'an alchemical cryptogram' which encodes Pope's 'mystical hope for a king who can restore the golden age'.

P57 Brown, Laura
ALEXANDER POPE (Oxford: 1985)

Part of Blackwell's *Re-Reading Literature* series, this book is an explicitly ideological attempt to reverse some conventional notions of Augustan values. Brown presents Pope's poetry as a series of hymns to consumer fetishism, paeans in praise of the new spirit of capitalist expansionism. Pope's irony is described as a form of mystification which veils but cannot hide his fascination with the monetary vices he condemns.

P58 Mack, Maynard
ALEXANDER POPE: A LIFE (New Haven, London: 1985)

As the culmination of his lifetime's study of Pope, Mack's biography is both fascinating and slightly disappointing. Mack's knowledge of Pope's life and work is unrivalled, yet in preparing this biography 'large amounts of detailed scholarly material' have been jettisoned – 'enough material', he concedes, 'to supply almost any number of other biographical studies'. As modern scholarly biographies go, this one is relatively brief, considering it is the first full-length biography of Pope for over fifty years. Mack's text runs to some 800 pages, but this includes at least a hundred illustrations and many pages of quotation. The portrait of Pope which emerges is highly sympathetic. Pope, Mack writes, 'has suffered too long from a species of self-righteousness in his commentators'. A theme that runs through the book is friendship. 'Pope has an unusual talent for friendship', says Mack. He deliberately sets out to make Pope popular and accessible to a large modern readership and the pages are filled with modern parallels and universal analogies. Discussing the 'disquieting narcissism' of Belinda in *The Rape of the Lock* he invites us to consider 'the late twentieth-century rock-star or professional athlete'.

Highly readable, a work of enthusiasm, insight and humanity.

P59   Pollak, Ellen
THE POETICS OF SEXUAL MYTH: GENDER AND
IDEOLOGY IN THE VERSE OF SWIFT AND POPE
(Chicago: 1985)

An excellent and original feminist reading of the verse of Pope and Swift. Through close verbal analysis, Pollak challenges many of the conventional 'New Critical' assumptions about these Augustan writers. Her study of the gendered vocabulary of *The Rape of the Lock* is particularly perceptive.

P60   Stack, Frank
POPE AND HORACE: STUDIES IN IMITATION
(Cambridge: 1985)

Stack argues that there is a vital and dynamic intertextual relationship between Horace's original poems and Pope's *Imitations*. Like Maresca (P23) he begins by asking how Horace was read in the eighteenth century, but unlike Maresca, rejects the idea that the Augustans favoured a largely 'Christianised' Horace. Introductory chapters on Horace and on imitation precede the detailed commentary on, and analysis of, the poems themselves. Erudite and precise, Stack places Pope's *Imitations* in a comparative context alongside versions of Horace by Dacier, Shaftesbury, Swift and others.

P61   Atkins, G. Douglas
       QUESTS OF DIFFERENCE, READING POPE'S POEMS
       (Lexington, Kentucky: 1986)

       An uneven and 'frankly exploratory' series of essays on the
       'reader-response' to Pope's poems. Sometimes pretentious,
       often banal, occasionally illuminating.

P62   Ferguson, Rebecca
       THE UNBALANCED MIND, POPE AND THE RULE
       OF PASSION (Brighton: 1986)

       A useful, unpretentious examination of the presentation of the
       passions in Pope's poetry. Particularly illuminating on *Eloisa to
       Abelard*.

P63   Hammond, Brean
       POPE (Brighton: Harvester New Readings, 1986)

       A lively if uneven study which sets out to reveal the ideological
       assumptions contained within Pope's moral and neo-classical
       axioms. Hammond is better on Pope's politics than on his
       poetry. He concludes with an avowedly feminist study of Pope's
       poems about women, which makes several interesting points
       while seeming unduly defensive. Highly readable.

P64   Berry, Reginald
       A POPE CHRONOLGY (London: 1988)

       A useful reference work, offering a clear chronology of Pope's
       career and setting his works in the context of contemporary
       public events. This is a strictly factual book which avoids
       biographical speculation and critical debate.

P65   Nicholson, Colin (ed.)
       ALEXANDER POPE, ESSAYS FOR THE
       TERCENTENARY (Aberdeen: 1988)

       This volume of fifteen commemorative essays is more notable
       for the generosity of its appreciation of Pope's work than for the
       originality of its research. Among the more significant contribu-
       tions are: 'Pope's Politics' (H. T. Dickinson); 'Pope and

Churchill' (Brean Hammond and Martin Malone); 'Pope, Money and Independence' (Ian A. Bell); and 'Text and Context: Pope's "Coronation Epistle" ' (W. W. Robson).

P66   Rousseau, G. S. and Pat Rogers (eds.)
THE ENDURING LEGACY, ALEXANDER POPE
TERCENTENARY ESSAYS (Cambridge: 1988)

An excellent and challenging collection of tercentenary essays. In the section 'Pope and Women', Felicity Rosslyn and Penelope Wilson take issue with recent feminist attacks on Pope. Rosslyn suggests analogies between Pope's depiction of the chameleon moods of women in the *Epistle to a Lady* and his descriptions of the transient rainbow tints of the poetic imagination. Wilson argues that feminist attitudes lead 'all too easily down a predominantly anachronistic and recriminatory cul-de-sac'. Howard Erskine-Hill provides a historical and philosophical context for understanding Pope's views on the origins and evolution of society, concluding that he 'found no conflict between the idea of patriarchalism and the idea of progress'. G. S. Rousseau offers a detailed and informative study of the politics of eighteenth-century humanism in an attempt to demystify the attitude to education expressed in *The Dunciad*. Pat Rogers speculates on similarities between Pope and Pushkin; David Morris discusses Pope and the arts of pleasure; Howard Weinbrot examines *The Rape of the Lock* and the contexts of warfare. The volume concludes with a characteristically energetic essay by Donald Greene on the history of critical attacks on Pope, entitled 'An Anatomy of Pope-bashing'.

Periodicals and Shorter Articles

P67   Johnson, Samuel
'The Life of Pope', THE LIVES OF THE ENGLISH
POETS (London: 1781)

Characteristically balanced, judicious and perceptive, Johnson describes Pope's life and work with sympathy, insight and critical detachment. Of the *Essay on Man* he remarks: 'Never were penury of knowledge and vulgarity of sentiment so happily disguised'. Elsewhere, he praises Pope's genius and imagination.

P68 Arnold, Matthew
Introduction to *The English Poets* (1880), reprinted as 'The
Study of Poetry' in ESSAYS IN CRITICISM, second series
(1888)

Probably the most celebrated example of damning Pope with
faint praise. Arnold's essay presents Pope as 'the splendid high
priest of our age of prose and reason'. It concludes that Pope
and Dryden lack 'the high seriousness . . . the poetic largeness,
freedom, insight and benignity' to be great poets. On the
contrary; 'Though they may write in verse, though they may in a
certain sense be masters cf the art of versification, Dryden and
Pope are not classics of our poetry, they are classics of our
prose'.

P69 Strachey, Lytton
'Pope', the Leslie Stephen Lecture for 1925 (Cambridge:
1925)

Witty and waspish, Strachey's essay combines repugnance for
the 'little monster of Twit'nam' with admiration for the monster's magical dexterity with the heroic couplet. Presents the
essence of Pope's art as antithesis. 'Antithesis penetrates below
the structure; it permeates the whole conception of his work.'

P70 Leavis, F. R.
'Pope', REVALUATION: TRADITION AND
DEVELOPMENT IN ENGLISH POETRY (London: 1936)

In this important essay Leavis detects a seriousness in Pope's
poetry that Arnold missed. 'The order of Augustan civilization
evokes characteristically in Pope, its poet, when he is moved by
the vision of it, a profound sense of it as dependent upon and
harmonious with an ultimate inclusive order.' Included in
Essential Articles, ed. Mack (P22).

Prior, Matthew (1664–1721)

PR1   Thackeray, W. M.
'Prior, Gay and Pope', THE ENGLISH HUMOURISTS OF
THE EIGHTEENTH CENTURY (London: 1853)

'Horace is always in his mind; and his song, and his philosophy,
his good sense, his happy easy turns and melody, his loves and
his Epicureanism, bear a great resemblance to that most de-
lightful and accomplished master.' Exuberant and impressionistic rather than critical.

PR2   Dobson, Austin (ed.)
SELECTED POEMS OF MATTHEW PRIOR (London:
1889)

In the course of his useful introductory essay Dobson argues
that Prior is 'as easy as Swift and as polished as Pope'.

PR3   Eves, Charles Kenneth
MATTHEW PRIOR, POET AND DIPLOMAT (New
York: 1973)

The first full-length scholarly biography. Eves has an unpreten-
tious style and he presents an interesting narrative as he traces
the precise connections between Prior's two public roles as poet
and diplomat.

Smart, Christopher (1722–71)

Editions

S1   Brittain, R. (ed.)
      POEMS BY CHRISTOPHER SMART (Princeton: 1950)

      An edition of the poems which includes a valuable seventy-
      four-page introduction, presenting an interesting survey of
      Smart's life and the changing critical fortunes of his work.
      Brittain is concerned to provide a common-sense interpretation
      of the man and to break away from the Romantic view of Smart
      as an insane poet.

S2   Walsh, Marcus (ed.)
      CHRISTOPHER SMART: SELECTED POEMS
      (Manchester: 1979)

      The brief introduction to this selection of Smart's poetry pro-
      vides a useful context for its understanding, which will be of
      particular interest to students unfamiliar with the material.

S3   Williamson, Karina
      THE POETICAL WORKS OF CHRISTOPHER SMART;
      Vol I, *JUBILATE AGNO* (Oxford: 1980)

      A critical edition of the poem which includes a concise introduc-
      tion to Smart's career, together with details of the discovery of
      the manuscript and its fragmentary condition.

Full-length Studies

S4   Ainsworth, E. G. and C. E. Noyes
      SMART: A BIOGRAPHICAL AND CRITICAL STUDY
      (Columbia, Missouri: 1943)

      The first full-length study in English of Smart's life and work.

Focuses on the growth of his religious belief to demonstrate the coherence of his development as a poet. Includes biographical material on Smart's relationship with Anne Vane, his career at college and in London, his marriage and his madness.

S5   Devlin, C.
POOR KIT SMART (London: 1961)

Devlin reads Smart as a misguided mystic, his self-created role as prophet pushing him into egotism instead of Christian humility. Provides an introductory review of the critical reception of Smart's poetry, and some (often speculative) biographical comments.

S6   Blaydes, S.
SMART AS A POET OF HIS TIMES: A REAPPRAISAL (The Hague: 1966)

Provides close readings of the major poems, tracing a coherent poetic development in the context of contemporary poetry. Offers little new information, however, and the thesis that Smart always followed literary conventions is dubious.

S7   Sherbo, Arthur
CHRISTOPHER SMART, SCHOLAR OF THE UNIVERSITY (East Lansing, Michigan: 1967)

Now the standard biography of Smart, largely superseding the work of Ainsworth and Noyes (S4). Sherbo incorporates much original information which his research has uncovered. He emphasises Smart's university career as a formative stage of his poetic development.

S8   Dearnley, M.
THE POETRY OF CHRISTOPHER SMART (London: 1968)

A careful, scholarly book which puts Smart's work into its contemporary context. Dearnley argues that Smart's secular poetry, though of little merit in itself, provides an essential background for the understanding of his religious works.

Periodicals and Shorter Articles

S9 Havens, Raymond D.
'The Structure of Smart's *Song to David*', *RES* 14 (1938)
178–82

Finds 'mystic numbers' in the structure of the poem, in the
grouping of lines into combinations of threes and sevens.
Suggests that each section of the poem corresponds to a formal
pattern, from the 'Invocation' through the repetition of key
words in successive stanzas, to an abrupt break with this in the
line 'The pillars of the lord are seven'. Sees Smart as 'the most
romantic' poet of his time in this poem, which is 'ecstatic,
sensuous, abrupt, and above all strange'.

S10 Greene, D. J. 'Smart, Berkeley, the Scientists and the Poets',
Journal of the History of Ideas 14 (June 1953) 327–52

Greene argues that, although Smart was interested in contemporary science, he anticipated Blake as 'the earliest of the
outright rebels against Newtonian and Lockean
"rationalism" '.

S11 Williamson, Karina
'Christopher Smart's *Hymns and Spiritual Songs*', *PQ* 38
(1959) 413–24

Explores the relationship between Smart's *Hymns and Spiritual
Songs* and the conventions of hymn-writing in the eighteenth
century, emphasising that, in the Anglican tradition of metrical
psalms, hymn-writing itself was 'an unorthodox, even eccentric, occupation'.

S12 Grigson, G.
CHRISTOPHER SMART, British Council pamphlet
(London: 1961)

Grigson provides a useful introduction to the life and works,
drawing on previous critical approaches, particularly
Ainsworth and Noyes (S4) and Sherbo (S7).

S13   Adams, Francis D.
'The Seven Pillars of Christopher Smart', *Papers on English
Language and Literature* I (1965) 125–32

Suggests that, on the basis of 'clues within the poem', Smart's
Song to David should be interpreted in the light of the 'seven
pillars of knowledge' conceit, so that 'David is the speaker in
the pillar stanzas and each of the pillars represents an individual
psalm'.

S14   Sherbo, Arthur
'Christopher Smart's Three Translations of Horace', *JEGP*
lxvi (1967) 347–58

Sherbo argues that Smart's translations of Horace deserve
serious critical attention.

S15   Hart, Edward
'Christopher Smart's Verse Satire', *Satire Newsletter* vi (1968)
29–34

Argues that, as a versatile poet in an age when satire was very
popular, Smart would be unlikely not to write any. In addition
to the satirical fables and the *Hilliad*, Hart finds satiric touches
throughout Smart's poetry, including the *Jubilate Agno* and the
Ode to General Draper. Suggests characteristic themes and
methods in Smart's satiric verses.

S16   Hope, A. D.
'The Apocalypse of Christopher Smart', STUDIES IN THE
EIGHTEENTH CENTURY, ed. R. F. Brissenden
(Canberra: 1968) 276–84

Hope suggests that *Jubilate Agno* contains 'a plan of reform'
which is so revolutionary as to border on an 'apocalyptic vision'.
Although the poem does not elaborate the theme, Hope argues
that it is based on a 'single fairly coherent theory of the
universe'.

S17   Davie, Donald
'Christopher Smart: Some Neglected Poems', *ECS* iii (1969)
242–64

Looks at Smart's *Hymns for the Amusement of Children*, his
versions of the Psalms and his translations of Horace.

S18   Parkin, Rebecca Price
'Christopher Smart's Sacramental Cat', *TSLL* xi (1969)
1191–6

Sees Smart's cat Jeoffry as a symbol of the divine.

S19   Wilkinson, Jean
'Three Sets of Religious Poems', *HLQ* 36 (1973) 203–26

Compares Smart's *Hymns and Spiritual Songs* with Herbert's
The Temple and Keble's *The Christian Year*. Ranks Smart as
Herbert's equal in religious poetry.

S20   Dennis, Christopher M.
'A Structural Conceit in Smart's *Song to David*', *RES* 29
(1978) 257–66

Analyses the poem as an example of Christian typology in the
exegetical tradition. Argues that, in the symbol of God the
Creator, Smart found 'a radical typology which suggests . . .
the unity of the world'.

Theobald, Lewis (1688–1744)

T1 Jones, Richard Foster
LEWIS THEOBALD, HIS CONTRIBUTION TO
ENGLISH SCHOLARSHIP (New York: 1919)

This excellent volume represents an important rehabilitation of
the reputation of Pope's King Dunce. Theobald's editorial
principles are carefully examined in the light of Bentley's
influence. An interesting sidelight on Augustan literary criticism. Judicious, scholarly and informative.

Thomson, James (1700–48)

Bibliographies

TH1   Campbell, Hilbert H.
JAMES THOMSON: AN ANNOTATED
BIBLIOGRAPHY OF SELECTED EDITIONS AND
IMPORTANT CRITICISM (New York, London: 1976)

An excellent source for the serious student of Thomson.

Full-length Studies

TH2   Macaulay, G. C.
JAMES THOMSON (London: 1908)

In its day, the standard biography of Thomson. Modern scholarship has challenged some of the dates and information.

TH3   McKillop, A. D.
THE BACKGROUND OF THOMSON'S *SEASONS*
(Minneapolis: 1942)

A highly influential study, setting *The Seasons* in the context of the philosophical and literary background, and tracing specific influences of philosophical scientific writings.

TH4   Grant, Douglas
JAMES THOMSON: POET OF 'THE SEASONS' (London: 1951)

A readable biography incorporating Grant's discovery of several letters from Thomson to Elizabeth Young (the 'Amanda' of the poems). Grant argues that the unrequited affair had a tragic effect on Thomson's personal life in the 1740s. The book also includes some critical commentary which is derived from the major Thomsonian critics, especially McKillop (TH3) and Nicolson (TH13).

TH5   Spacks, Patricia Meyer
THE VARIED GOD: A CRITICAL STUDY OF
THOMSON'S 'THE SEASONS' (Berkeley: 1959)

A valuable study, which sees the rewriting of *The Seasons* as evidence of Thomson's 'consistent general progression' away from nature and towards interest in human affairs. Spacks argues that this was a retrogressive step for Thomson's poetic development.

TH6   Cohen, Ralph
THE ART OF DISCRIMINATION: THOMSON'S 'THE
SEASONS' AND THE LANGUAGE OF CRITICISM
(London: 1964)

As the title suggests, this is a study of critical responses to *The Seasons* rather than of the poem itself. Cohen takes Thomson's poem as a model to test some general assumptions about literary and critical comment in the eighteenth century, and continues with a history of critical attitudes down to 1950.

TH7   Cohen, Ralph
THE UNFOLDING OF 'THE SEASONS': A STUDY OF
JAMES THOMSON'S POEM (Baltimore: 1970)

In this study, Cohen approaches Thomson as an English Augustan rather than as a forerunner of the Romantics. Cohen offers a close reading of *The Seasons* through a detailed study of imagery, syntax and vocabulary. He interprets the poem's apparent disjunctions as a deliberate device reflecting man's perceptions of worldly transience; behind this, Cohen argues, nature manifests Christian order.

TH8   Campbell, Hilbert H.
JAMES THOMSON, Twayne *English Authors* series
(Boston: 1979)

Campbell divides his material into three sections: *The Seasons*, other writings, and Thomson's life. In the biographical section he includes comment on Thomson's critical reputation and influence. Within the constraints of the series, Campbell offers a concise and accurate, if not particularly stimulating, introduction to Thomson. The discussion of *The Seasons* usefully summarises recent critical opinions, and the bibliography provides a handy reference guide for the student.

Periodicals

TH9 Hamilton, Horace E.
'James Thomson's *Seasons*: Shifts in the Treatment of Popular Subject Matter', *ELH* 15 (1948) 110–21

Traces the shift away from popular spectacle towards scientific realism in the revised version of *The Seasons*.

TH10 McKillop, A. D.
'Thomson and the Jail Committee', *SP* xlvii (1950) 62–71

Useful comments on contemporary philanthropy, and Thomson's interest in the Jail Committee of 1729.

References to Thomson in Other Works

TH11 Thompson, Alexander H.
THOMSON AND NATURAL DESCRIPTION IN POETRY, *Cambridge History of English Literature*, vol. 10 (1913)

A general essay of an introductory nature which should only be consulted in conjunction with more recent studies.

TH12 Mackail, J. W.
'The Poet of *The Seasons*', STUDIES OF ENGLISH POETS (New York: 1926) 83–109

Although Mackail's critical method now seems very dated, the discussion of Thomson's life and work is interesting. Comments on the dramas and shorter lyrics as well as the major poems.

TH13 Nicolson, Marjorie Hope
      NEWTON DEMANDS THE MUSE: NEWTON'S
      OPTICKS AND THE EIGHTEENTH-CENTURY POETS
      (Princeton: 1946)

Nicolson argues that eighteenth-century poets were more familiar with Newton's *Opticks* than with his *Principia*. She
presents Thomson as a major 'Newtonian' poet. A highly
significant and interesting approach to Thomson.

TH14 McKillop, A. D.
      'Ethics and Political History in Thomson's "Liberty" ',
      POPE AND HIS CONTEMPORARIES: ESSAYS
      PRESENTED TO GEORGE SHERBURN (Oxford: 1949)
      215–29

Links Thomson's account of political history with parallels
ranging from Plutarch to Rapin-Thoyras. McKillop also suggests that 'Liberty' shares some common ground with the
opposition journal of the 1730s, *The Craftsman*.

TH15 Butt, John
      'Thomson', THE AUGUSTAN AGE (1950; reprinted New
      York, 1966) 75–95

Butt comments on Thomson's use of the sublime, and his
'Newtonian' vision.

TH16 Price, Martin
      'The Theatre of Nature: James Thomson', TO THE
      PALACE OF WISDOM: STUDIES IN ORDER AND
      ENERGY FROM DRYDEN TO BLAKE (New York:
      1964) 351–61

Price argues that *The Seasons* operates by means of a dual
perspective in human and divine; as God reaches down to man
in plentitude, man ascends as he recognises divine order. The
subject of the poem, Price argues, is not the poet but the
principle of order in the created world; behind this, the shifting
structure of the poem mirrors the processes of the associative
human mind.

TH17 Cohen, Ralph
'Thomson's Poetry of Space and Time', STUDIES IN
CRITICISM AND AESTHETICS 1660–1800 (ed. Anderson,
Howard and John S. Shea) (Minneapolis: 1967) 176–92

Discusses Thomson's use of georgic conventions in his presentation of cyclical change in *The Seasons*, and argues that Thomson imaginatively 'departed from precedent and sought new expressions for space and time'. On occasion, Cohen argues, these experiments were disastrous, producing inappropriate linguistic and metaphorical combinations.

TH18 Spacks, Patricia Meyer
'James Thomson: The Retreat from Vision', THE POETRY
OF VISION (Cambridge: 1967) 46–65

Spacks argues that *The Castle of Indolence* presents an emotional rather than an intellectual or visual experience.

TH19 Chalker, John
'Thomson's Seasons', THE ENGLISH GEORGIC
(Baltimore: 1969) 90–140

An excellent discussion of *The Seasons*, arguing that the complexities of the poem are clarified when it is related to the Virgilian tradition. Chalker particularly suggests Virgil's georgics as an influence, blending an ideal past with pride in the present.

Tickell, Thomas (1685–1740)

TI1   Tickell, R. E.
THOMAS TICKELL AND THE EIGHTEENTH-
CENTURY POETS (London: 1931)

Compiled from family papers, this is essentially a rescue work.
Quoting a large number of letters, Tickell (R. E.) seeks to
establish his ancestor as a conscientious poet and public ser-
vant, unjustly pilloried by Pope. Many factual points of interest, but the literary criticism is negligible.

Waller, Edmund (1606–87)

W1   Allison, Alexander Ward
      TOWARDS AN AUGUSTAN POETIC: EDMUND
      WALLER'S 'REFORM' OF ENGLISH POETRY
      (Lexington, Kentucky: 1962)

      Allison claims that Waller 'waged a mild but direct campaign'
      against the conventions of Jacobean eulogy. An accurate sur-
      vey of Waller's poetic style, although some of his critical
      emphases are idiosyncratic.

W2   Chernaik, Warren L.
      THE POETRY OF LIMITATIONS (New Haven: 1968)

      The first full-length critical study of Waller, the poet regarded
      by contemporaries and ever since as 'the first Augustan'.
      Chernaik's term 'limitations' indicates both a sense of discipline
      and of renunciation in the poetry. He concludes: 'His art is a
      cautious art of limitations, but within these limitations he was
      able to do a few things very well'. A valuable study of this
      influential but neglected poet.

Walpole, Horace (1717–97)

WA1　Ketton-Cremer, R. W.
WALPOLE: A BIOGRAPHY (1940; revised 1946; 3rd edn
London: 1964)

A useful and readable biography of Walpole for both the
specialist and the general reader. The third edition is not a
substantial revision, but does correct some errors in the earlier
printings.

WA2　Honour, Hugh
HORACE WALPOLE, *Writers and Their Works* series
(London: 1957)

A brief introduction to the life and works of Walpole for the
student unfamiliar with either.

WA3　Lewis, Wilmarth S.
HORACE WALPOLE (London: 1961)

A collection of six lectures given in the A. W. Mellon Lectures
in the Fine Arts, 1960. These hour-long papers are reproduced
without amplification, and offer a sympathetic and highly
knowledgeable account of Walpole the man. The first essay
provides a survey of Walpole's family background; further
papers throw light on the Strawberry Hill set, Walpole's political activities, his works and letters. The volume also includes an
excellent selection of portraits of Walpole throughout his life.

WA4　Smith, Warren Hunting (ed.)
HORACE WALPOLE: WRITER, POLITICIAN AND
CONNOISSEUR, ESSAYS ON THE TWO HUNDRED
AND FIFTIETH ANNIVERSARY OF WALPOLE'S
BIRTH (New Haven: 1967)

A collection of nineteen essays, wide-ranging, elegant and

informative. Of interest to students of literature are Robert Halsband, 'Walpole versus Lady Mary'; C. B. Hogan, 'The Theatre of George III' (on the plays and *The Castle of Otranto*); J. M. Osborn, 'Horace Walpole and Edmund Malone'; and Frederick Pottle on the part played by Walpole and Boswell in the quarrel between Rousseau and Hume. Other essays range from Walpole's politics to his idiosyncratic taste in antiquities.

WA5   Lewis, Wilmarth S.
RESCUING HORACE WALPOLE (New Haven, London: 1979)

Lewis, a lifetime collector of Walpole books and manuscripts, has amassed a private collection of unparalleled stature. His academic attention to the manuscripts and publications is a major contribution to Walpole scholarship; this book is a light-hearted account of his adventures in tracing the material. Anecdotal and entertaining, it describes the international wheeler-dealing of book traders and collectors, an aspect of literary life rarely visible in academic treatises. The items listed also demonstrate Walpole's wide range of interests, his friend-ships and the chronology of his life.

WA6   Fothergill, Brian
THE STRAWBERRY HILL SET: HORACE WALPOLE AND HIS CIRCLE (London: 1983)

Walpole celebrated Twickenham as 'the Muses fav'rite seat' – the Gothic revival centres on the collaborative atmosphere of Strawberry Hill. A good introduction to Walpole for the general reader, though less useful than W. S. Lewis's *Horace Walpole* (WA3).

Warton, Joseph (1722–1800)
Warton, Thomas (c. 1688–1745)
Warton, Thomas (1728–90)

Full-length Studies

WR1   Partridge, Eric (ed.)
THE THREE WARTONS, A CHOICE OF THEIR
VERSE (London: 1927)

A selection of poems by the three Wartons, with heavy emphasis on the romantic elements of their work. Partridge notes
that all three poets show a marked family resemblance of theme
and style.

WR2   Pittock, Joan
THE ASCENDANCY OF TASTE: THE ACHIEVEMENT
OF JOSEPH AND THOMAS WARTON (London: 1973)

More about concepts of 'taste' than about the Wartons, Pittock's book analyses the term throughout the eighteenth century. The last two chapters locate the Wartons in this context.

Periodicals and Shorter Articles

WR3   Gosse, Edmund W.
'Two Pioneers of Romanticism: Joseph and Thomas Warton',
Warton Lecture on English Poetry No. 6 (London: 1915)

A brief paper displaying Gosse's characteristically eloquent
and idiosyncratic critical approach. More interesting as an
example of early-twentieth-century criticism than as a serious
approach to the poetry of the Wartons.

WR4 Bishop, David H.
'The Father of the Wartons', *SAQ* xvi (1917) 357–8

Interprets Thomas Warton the Elder as a pioneer Romantic, anticipating the work of his sons despite his contemporary context in 'the hey-day of Pope'. An example of the critical interpretations of Thomas Warton challenged by David Fairer (WR11).

WR5 Havens, Raymond D.
'Thomas Warton and the Eighteenth-Century Dilemma', *SP* xxv (1928) 36–50

A useful reading of Warton's texts, and an excellent critique of the changing aesthetic theories behind Warton's essay on the *Faerie Queene*.

WR6 Martin, Louis C.
'Thomas Warton and the Early Poems of Milton', Warton Lecture on English Poetry (London: 1934)

A brief study in stylistic and ideational indebtedness.

WR7 Kirschbaum, Leo
'The Imitations of Thomas Warton the Elder', *PQ* 22 (1943) 119–24

Kirschbaum sees Thomas Warton as 'a conscious experimenter, purposefully engaged in enlarging the bounds of poetry'.

WR8 Hysham, Julia
'Joseph Warton's Reputation as a Poet', *Studies in Romanticism* I (1962) 220–9

Surveys the changing reputation of Warton's poetry, from the opinions of contemporaries such as William Collins, through the tendency of late-nineteenth- and early-twentieth-century critics to read his works as the precursors of Romanticism. Concludes that Warton's verses are best read as a distinctive voice, separate from either Augustanism or the Romantics.

WR9   Griffith, Philip Malone
'Joseph Warton's Criticism of Shakespeare', *Tulane Studies in English* xiv (1965) 17–56

An interesting approach to Warton's role in changing literary tastes and scholarly perceptions of earlier English literature.

WR10   Morris, David B.
'Joseph Warton's Figure of Virtue: Poetic Indirection in "The Enthusiast" ', *PQ* 50 (October 1971) 678–83

A brief article on Warton's 1744 poem *The Enthusiast or The Lover of Nature*, demonstrating Warton's use of classical allegory and allusion.

WR11   Fairer, David
'The Poems of Thomas Warton the Elder', *RES* n.s. 26 (1975) 287–300, 395–406

Presents Fairer's findings on the authorship of verses in Thomas Warton's posthumously published *Poems on Several Occasions* (1748). Fairer has established that six of the poems are actually by his son Joseph and four by his son Thomas; a further two poems were substantially revised by Joseph. The significance of Fairer's discovery is that it demands an important reassessment of the achievements of the Warton family; earlier critics had seen Thomas Warton the Elder as a pioneer of Romanticism, influencing the taste for the primitive displayed by his sons, but Fairer proves that his sons were the true innovators.

WR12   Le Prevost, Christina
'More Unacknowledged Verse by Joseph Warton', *RES* n.s. 37 (1986) 317–47

'More' refers to the discoveries made by David Fairer in an earlier issue of RES (WR11). Le Prevost's article continues Fairer's important work of reattributing the verses, on the basis of manuscript evidence.

Young, Edward (1683–1765)

Full-length Studies

Y1   Shelley, Henry Charles
THE LIFE AND LETTERS OF EDWARD YOUNG
(London: 1914)

A limited but useful early biography.

Y2   Clark. H. H.
THE ROMANTICISM OF EDWARD YOUNG (Madison:
1929, reprinted from the Transactions of Wisconsin
Academy, vol. 24, Nov. 1929)

Clark measures Young's 'romanticism' against the Romantics,
discovering twelve 'major traits' which they share. Clark's
critical method is that of the Irving Babbitt school characterised
by undefined phrases such as 'True Christian Aspiration'. One
quote will suffice: 'It is scarcely necessary to remark that here
we stand at the headwaters of a current which was to sweep with
devastating violence over the war-torn fields of France in 1917'.

Y3   Wicker, C. V.
EDWARD YOUNG AND THE FEAR OF DEATH: A
STUDY IN ROMANTIC MELANCHOLY (Albuquerque,
Mexico: 1952)

'Let's talk of graves, of worms and epitaphs' Wicker quotes
from *Richard II* as the keynote of his study. 'Painfully, fran-
tically', he argues, Young 'strove to teach himself how to die.'
Seeking death in every verse from the minor poems to *The
Night Thoughts*, he argues that Young was in the 'Graveyard
tradition', along with the poets Parnell, Thomas Warton and
Gray. Essentially sees Young as a brooding forerunner of the
Romantics, obsessed with death and melancholy solitude, and
his poetry as offering 'the contemplation of death, terror,
horror, fear, deep gloom, or resignation'.

Y4   Bliss, Isabel St John
      EDWARD YOUNG, Twayne *English Authors* series (New
      York: 1969)

      Bliss's biography of Young is brief but reliable, and her critical
      commentary, within the limits of the Twayne series, is
      perceptive.

Y5   Forster, Harold
      EDWARD YOUNG: THE POET OF *THE NIGHT
      THOUGHTS*, 1683–1765 (Alburgh, Harleston, Norfolk:
      1987)

      In this posthumously published biography, Forster traces the
      changing popular estimations of Young's poetry from the
      height of its critical reception in the eighteenth century through
      to the disgust of the Romantics and George Eliot. Forster
      provides a well researched and factually accurate account of
      Young's life, although his critical approach to the poetry is
      highly idiosyncratic. Reading Young not as an Augustan but as
      a poet of sensibility born before his time, Forster fails to link
      Young to contemporary conventions.

Periodicals

Y6   Bliss, Isabel St John
      'Young's "Night Thoughts" in Relation to Contemporary
      Christian Apologetics', *PMLA* 1934 xlix 37–70

      Bliss argues that, while it is important to look at the 'so-called
      personal element and the treatment of the theme of death',
      Young's *Night Thoughts* cannot be understood without the
      context of contemporary Christian apologetics. Her article
      provides a useful and perceptive study.

Y7   Odell, Daniel W.
      'Young's *Night Thoughts* as an Answer to Pope's *Essay on
      Man*', *SEL* 12 (1972) 481–501

      Odell argues that Young's own philosophy, and his conception
      of Pope's poem, is revealed in the way each poem 'confronts
      man's nature and place in the chain of being and the problem of
      evil'.

Index of Authors

Index of Subjects